Phonics Made Simple

Kindergarten

Written by Vicky Shiotsu
Illustrated by Mark Mason and Becky Radtke

Notice! Copies of student pages may be reproduced by the classroom teacher for classroom use only, not for commercial resale. No part of this publication may be reproduced for storage in a retrieval system, or transmitted in any form or by any means—electronic, mechanical, recording, etc.—without the prior written permission of the publisher. Reproduction of these materials for an entire school or school system is strictly prohibited.

FS123306 Phonics Made Simple—Kindergarten
All rights reserved–Printed in the U.S.A.
Copyright © 2000 Frank Schaffer Publications, Inc.
23740 Hawthorne Blvd.
Torrance, CA 90505

Editor: Jeanine Manfro
Art Director: Anthony Paular
Graphic Artist: Randy Shinsato

Table of Contents

Introduction	**1**
The Alphabet	**2–12**
Identification and Sequence	2–8
Sounds of the Alphabet	9
Writing the Alphabet	10–12
Consonants	**13–64**
General Activities for Beginning Consonants	13–15
Individual Consonants	16–57
Review Beginning Consonants	58–60
General Activities for Final Consonants	61–64
Short Vowels	**65–76**
General Activities	65
Individual Vowels	66–75
Short Vowel Review	76
Answer Key	77–78

Introduction

Phonics is an important tool for understanding how written English "works." As children learn about the relationship between sounds and letters, they see that how a word is read or written is based on certain systematic rules.

There are 26 letters of the alphabet.

Many consonants only make one sound.

The sounds of vowels vary.

Learning phonics is an important step in learning how to read and write.

Reading and writing are essential skills of communication. An important part of acquiring these skills comes from a knowledge of phonetic rules and an understanding of how written English "works." *Phonics Made Simple—Kindergarten* is designed to help teachers plan a phonics program that helps children become aware of the relationship between the letters of the alphabet and the sounds of English. The activities in this book incorporate a variety of sensory experiences—visual aids, movement activities, poems, creative writing, and more—to make learning phonics both stimulating and rewarding. As students develop the ability to identify letters and to discriminate consonant and vowel sounds, they will be excited to learn that they can apply these skills in order to "figure out" what a word says or how to write words on their own. These early successes in reading and writing are crucial in the development of a child's self-confidence and self-esteem, and they lay the foundation for future learning.

Phonics Made Simple—Kindergarten can be used alone or as an integral part of any language arts program. The book is divided into three sections: *The Alphabet, Consonants,* and *Short Vowels*. Each section presents a variety of activities that are interesting, challenging, and age-appropriate. The activities in each section may be introduced sequentially as they appear in the book or in random order.

The Alphabet

The alphabet is the foundation of written English. Most children entering school are familiar with the letters of the alphabet because of the influence of preschool as well as the exposure to educational TV and video programs, concept books, and learning-oriented toys. Kindergarten teachers can build on these early experiences by presenting a variety of activities that help children become aware of the relationship between the letters of the alphabet and the sounds of English, thereby laying the groundwork for beginning reading and writing.

CONCEPTS

The ideas and activities presented in this section will help children develop the following skills:

- identifying letters of the alphabet
- recognizing the sequence of letters
- matching uppercase and lowercase letters
- learning that letters are associated with sounds
- writing the alphabet

ALPHABET SONG — *Song*

Help your class practice saying the letters of the alphabet by singing the "Alphabet Song" every so often with them. Display an alphabet chart nearby, and point to the letters as you sing. Vary the song by occasionally changing the last two lines, as in the following example:

♪ A, B, C, D, E, F, G,

♪ H, I, J, K, L, M, N, O, P,

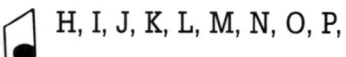

♪ W, X, Y, and Z.

♪ Now we know our ABC's,

Let's all clap for you and me!

Invite your students to make up their own endings to the song and let them teach the new versions to the class.

ALPHABET CATCH — *Game*

Play this catching game with a small group or the whole class. Begin by taking the children outdoors on the playground. Have the students stand in a circle with you in the middle. Then call out *A* and toss a ball to a student, letting the ball bounce once. The child who catches the ball calls out *B* and tosses the ball back to you. Say *C* and bounce the ball to another student. Continue the procedure until the entire alphabet has been recited.

Variation: Say a letter and bounce the ball to a student. The child then must say a word beginning with that letter before bouncing the ball back to you. (Play this version only after your class has had a chance to learn the sounds of vowels and consonants.)

NAME GRAPH

Class Activity

Here's a fun way for your class to compare what names begin with which letters. First, write each child's name on a flashcard. Make the first letter a different color from the others. Then give each child his or her name card.

Next, write the uppercase letters on individual cards. Mount the cards on butcher paper to create a long horizontal chart. Then have each child glue his or her name card under the letter that shows what letter his or her name begins with. Have the class answer questions such as the following: How many children have names that begin with *A*? Are there any children that have names that begin with *C*? Which do we have more of—names that begin with *L* or names that begin with *S*?

 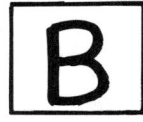 
  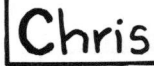

MANIPULATIVE LETTERS

Collect the lids of one-gallon plastic milk jugs. (Parents may be able to donate some to your class.) Then write a letter on each cap. Use the caps for the following activities:

- Place a complete set of letters in a self-sealing plastic bag. Have students take turns arranging the letters in sequence.

- Make a set of uppercase letters and lowercase letters, and let students match each uppercase letter with its lowercase counterpart.

- Challenge students to arrange the letters to spell out names or simple words. Have the children display their work on foam trays that can be shared with the class.

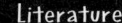
Literature

An Alphabet Tree

Read the delightful *Chicka Chicka Boom Boom,* by Bill Martin Jr. and John Archambault (Simon & Schuster, 1989), to the class. In this story, the letters of the alphabet race to the top of a coconut tree.

As you read the book, invite your students to join you in chanting the story's rhythmic refrain. Afterwards, draw a large palm tree on a sheet of chart paper. Then let each child draw and color a letter on a piece of paper. Have the students cut out the letters and glue them to the top of the tree.

ALPHABET CARDS

Class Activities

The alphabet cards presented on pages 5 and 6 have a variety of uses. Reproduce the pages on construction paper or heavy paper. (For some activities, every student will need a copy of the alphabet.) Then have the students cut out the cards and store each set in a self-sealing plastic bag. Use the following ideas as springboards for your own class activities:

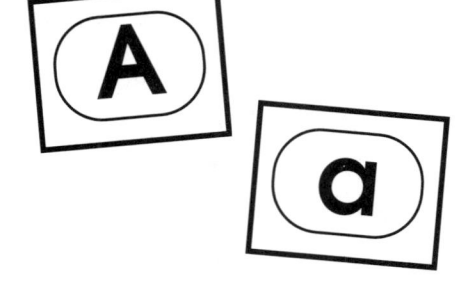

Listen and Find

Have each student lay out one set of cards on a table or on the floor. Then call out a letter. The students must find the letter you chose.

Alphabet Relay

Divide the class into three or more teams. Place a set of letters in a separate tray or a shallow box for each team. Have each team stand in a line several feet away from its alphabet set. Then call out a letter. The first person in line for each team must run to the alphabet set and find the letter you called. Those players then run back to their teams with the cards. Next, call out another letter; the second person in line for each team then runs and finds the corresponding card. Continue the procedure until every child has had a chance to find a letter.

Alphabet Bingo

Give each student a sheet of paper that has been divided into a 3 x 3 grid. Instruct the students to write or glue a letter in each box to make bingo cards consisting of nine letters. (Have the class work only with the uppercase letters or the lowercase letters.) Next, place a set of alphabet cards in a paper lunch bag. Begin the game by drawing a card and saying the name of the letter. If students have that letter, they cover it with a counter. (Use beans, small paper squares, buttons, or other small items for counters.) Continue the activity until a student has covered all nine letters of his or her bingo card. That child wins the game and becomes the new caller.

Alphabet Scavenger Hunt

Tape one set of alphabet cards in various places around the room. Then give each student a copy of page 5 or 6 (uncut) as a checkoff list. Tell the children to walk around the room and look for the letters. As each letter is found, it is checked off on the alphabet page. Play the game until all the students have succeeded in finding the entire alphabet.

Alphabet Cards

A	B
C	D	E	F
G	H	I	J
K	L	M	N
O	P	Q	R
S	T	U	V
W	X	Y	Z

Alphabet Cards

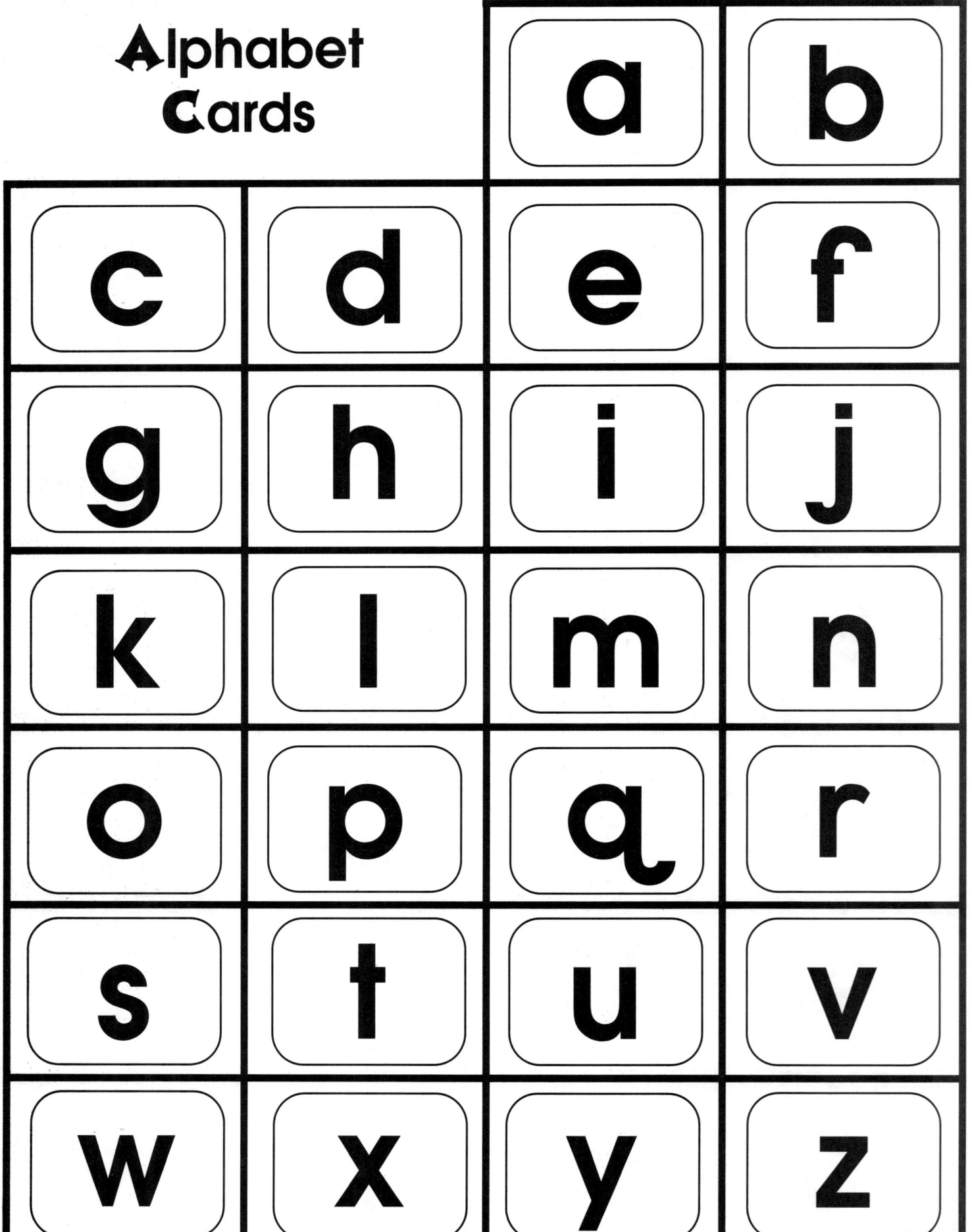

MEMORY MATCH

Matching Game

Make a memory match game by reproducing the letters on pages 5 and 6. Cut the letters apart and glue them onto index cards. Separate the cards into three sets: *A–I; J–R; S–Z.* Put each set in an envelope or self-sealing plastic bag. Let small groups of children play with a set at a time.

To play the game, all the cards in a set are laid facedown on a table or the floor. Players take turns picking up two cards at a time. If the cards display an uppercase letter and its lowercase counterpart, the player keeps the cards. The player then picks up another pair of cards. If a match is not made, the next player takes a turn. After all the cards have been picked up, the player with the most cards wins.

Variation: Reproduce two sets of uppercase or lowercase letters. Have the students match like letters together.

FISHING FOR LETTERS

Group Activity

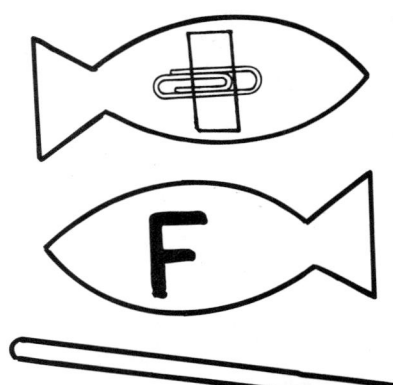

Cut out fish shapes from paper. Write a letter on one side of each fish and tape a paper clip to the other side. Make a fishing pole by tying string to the end of a yardstick or dowel. Tie a magnet to the end of the string. Then lay the fish on the floor, with the paper clips facing up. Let small groups of students take turns "catching" a fish. When a student catches a fish, he or she looks at the letter and says it aloud.

Variation: Have students say a word that begins with the letter on the fish.

THE ALPHABET TRAIN

Class Activity

Here's a fun way for your class to practice sequencing the alphabet. Reproduce a copy of the alphabet train (page 8) for every student. As the children look at the letters on the train, have them say the alphabet with you. Then discuss the different passengers and objects on the train. Have the students say the names, and point out the beginning sound of each word. For example, have the students notice that the train's engineer is an alligator and that *alligator* begins with *A*.

Next, instruct the children to cut along the heavy lines on the page. (Each child will get eight pieces.) Have the students shuffle the pieces to put them out of order. Then let the children work at a long table or on the floor to see how long it takes them to put their trains in order. Afterwards, have them store their pieces in an envelope or self-sealing plastic bag for future use.

Variation: Reproduce several sets of the alphabet train on heavy paper. Store each set in an envelope or a plastic bag. Leave the sets at a center where small groups of children can work on the puzzles.

The Alphabet Train

Cut out the train. Put the cars in ABC order. Store the pieces so that you can play with them again.

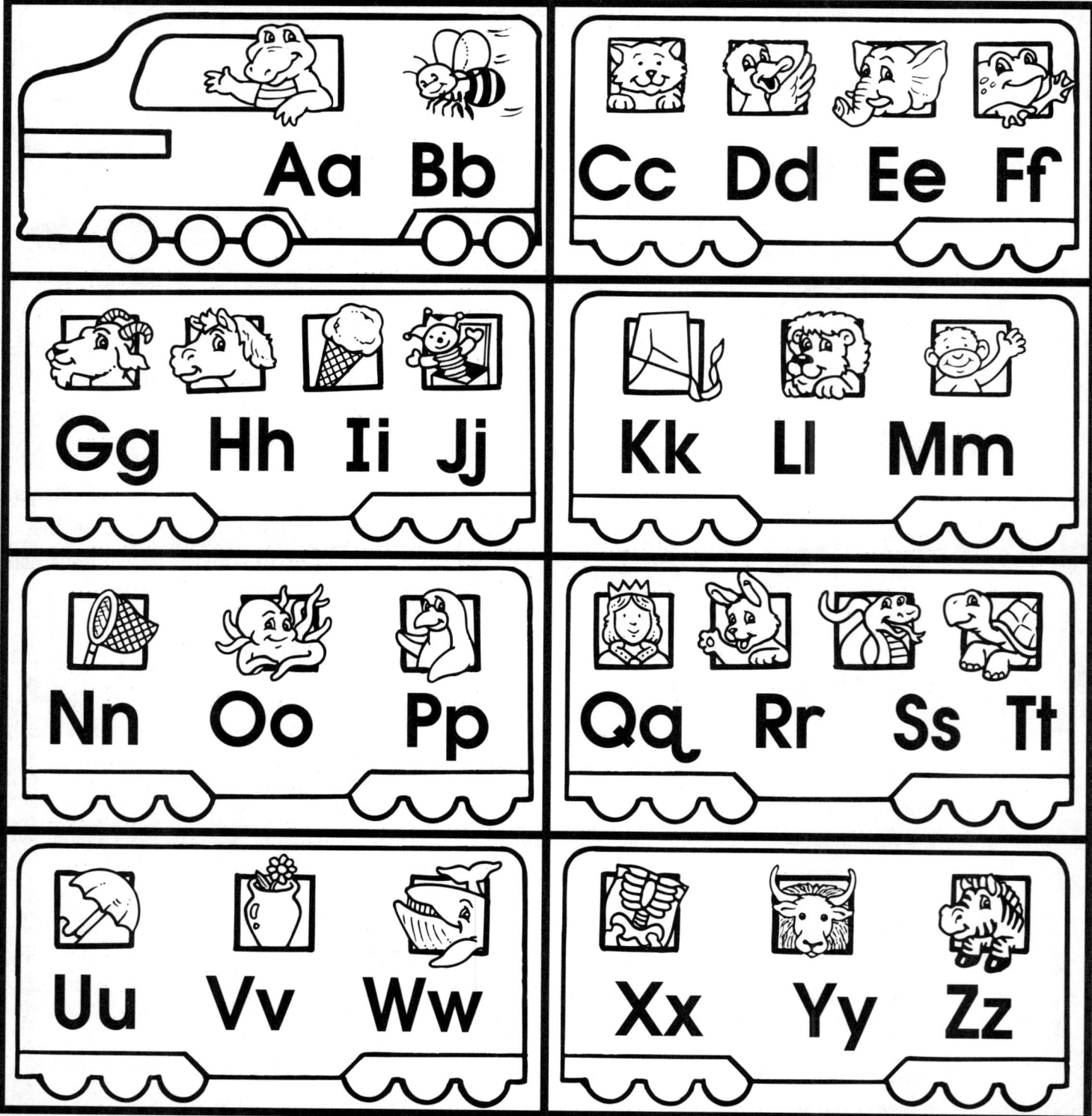

A LIFT-THE-FLAP BOOK OF SOUNDS

Class Activity

There are a variety of alphabet books in which the child reads a letter on a flap and then lifts the flap to discover a picture that begins with that letter. Two such books are Chuck Murphy's *My First Book of the Alphabet* (Scholastic, 1992) and David Pelham's *A Is for Animals* (Simon & Schuster, 1991). Read these or other lift-the-flap books and have your students guess the picture before lifting each flap. Afterwards, let your students make a similar alphabet book in class.

To make the pages in the book, first get 26 sheets of white paper and 26 six-inch squares of construction paper. Write a letter (both uppercase and lowercase) on each square. Then tape the top of a square to the middle of each sheet of white paper.

Give each student a page of the book. Have the children carefully lift and fold the flaps back, and then draw an appropriate picture underneath. (If you like, discuss with the class ahead of time the kinds of pictures they could draw for each letter.) After the students have drawn and colored their pictures, arrange the pages in alphabetical order. Add construction paper covers, and then staple or bind the papers together.

ALPHABET CHANT

Class Activity

This activity provides a perfect transition when your class has a few minutes to spare. Students begin by sitting in their chairs. Then say the following chant together, clapping out the rhythm as you go:

All sit together, class,

Let's say the alphabet,

When it's your letter, you must stand up!

Then state the letters of the alphabet, clapping as you say each one. When a student hears the letter that his or her name begins with, he or she must stand up. By the end of the alphabet, all the students will be standing.

Next, repeat the chant, but this time have the students sit down when they hear their letters. By the end of the activity, all the students will be sitting back in their chairs.

WRITING FUN

Writing Activity

As your students become familiar with the alphabet, they will also practice writing the letters. Here are some fun alternatives to using traditional handwriting paper with the class:

- Set out a tub of wet sand, a new unsharpened pencil, a toy shovel, and some letter cards. Let the children practice copying letters in the sand. Instruct them to "erase" the letters by smoothing the sand out with the shovel. For an extra challenge, set out some word cards and have the students copy words in the sand.

Game

- Have the students stamp out letters using rubber stamps. Tell the class to stamp the letters on the top half of a sheet of paper. Then instruct the students to copy the letters with pencil on the bottom half of the paper.

- Let small groups of children practice writing on the chalkboard. Display an alphabet chart nearby, or write on the board the individual letters that you want the class to practice.

WHAT'S THE LETTER?

Pair up the children for this quick and easy guessing game. To play, one partner "writes" a letter with his or her finger on the other partner's back. If the partner guesses the letter, the two children switch roles. If not, the student gets two more chances to guess before changing places.

Variation: Have one child close his or her eyes while the partner "writes" a letter in the child's hand.

HEAR AND WRITE

Class Activity

Use this activity to get a quick assessment of your students' abilities to write letters. Give each child a sheet of paper and show the class how to fold the paper into fourths. Then say a letter, and have the students write it in the top left-hand section of their paper. Say a different letter, and have the children write it in the top right-hand section. Repeat the procedure two more times until the class has written four letters on the paper. Give children who had difficulties extra opportunities to practice writing letters in class. (See "Writing Fun" activity above.)

LETTER PERFECT

Writing Activity

Reproduce pages 11 and 12 as an alphabet review for the class. After the students have completed the assignments, give each of them a file folder in which to glue the papers. Let the children keep their folders at their desks for future reference.

Name _____

Letters on Parade

Trace the letters. Then say their names.

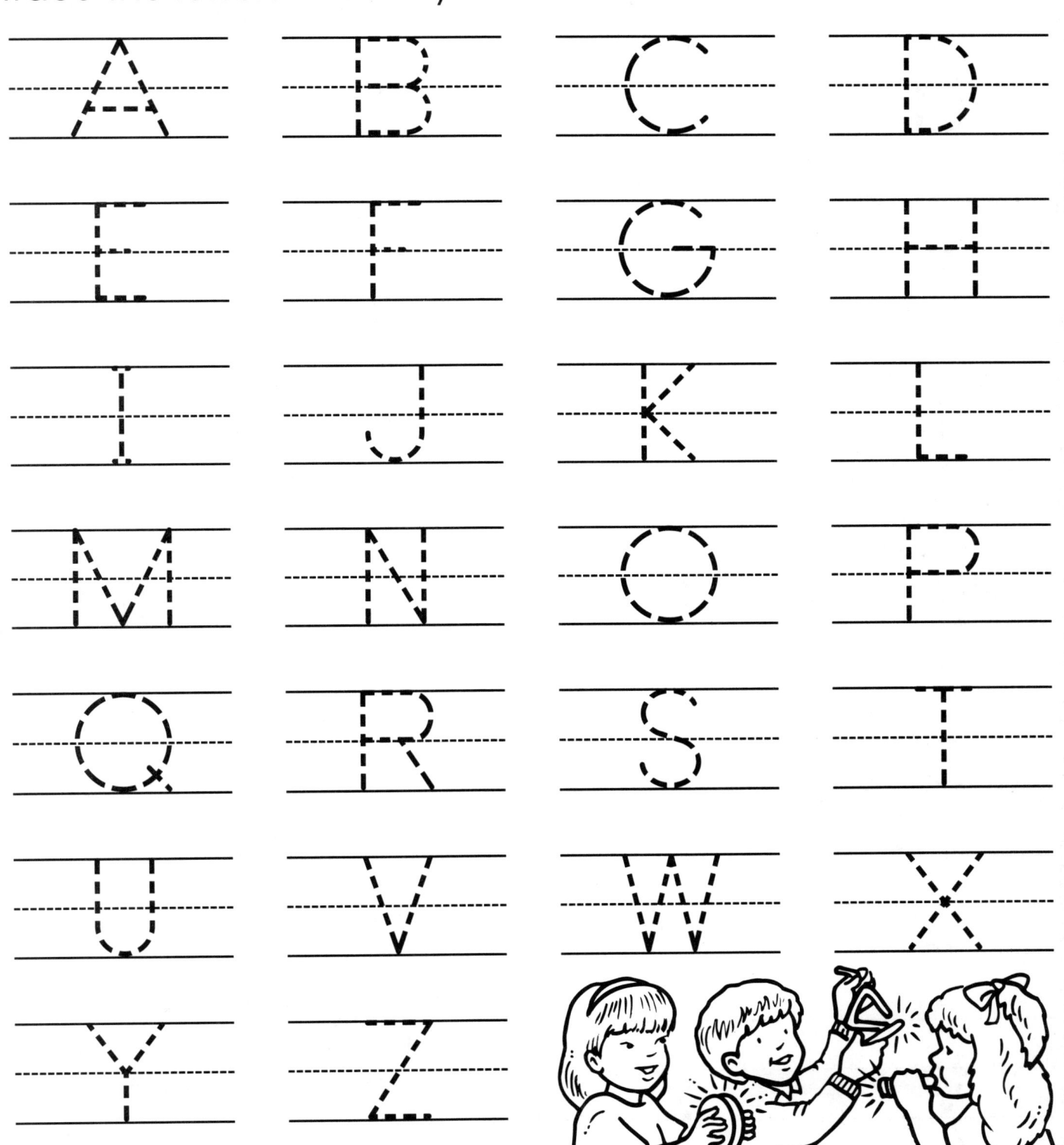

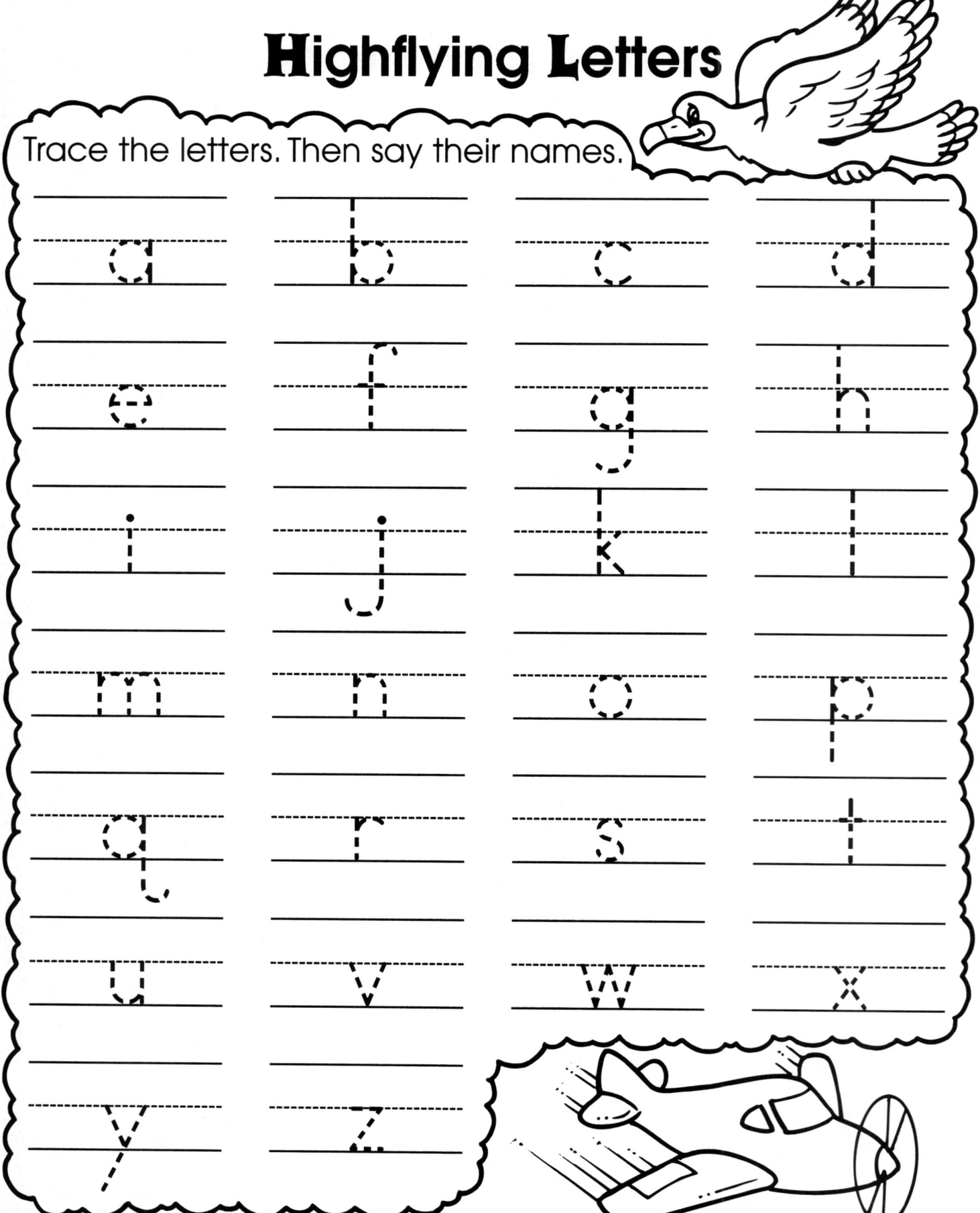

Consonants

Distinguishing the sounds of the consonants can be thought of as the "jumping-off" point from which young children begin learning how to read and write. Consonants produce sounds that are more consistent and more easily identifiable than vowels. When children learn to recognize the sounds of consonants (in both the beginning and final positions of words), they gain the ability to look at a word and make reasonable guesses as to what it might be. Helping children acquire a knowledge of consonants is essential to helping them understand how written English "works."

CONCEPTS

The ideas and activities presented in this section will help children develop the following skills:

- identifying beginning consonant sounds
- distinguishing between two or more beginning consonants
- identifying final consonant sounds
- distinguishing between two or more final consonants
- choosing words that have a particular beginning or final consonant

Organization

WHAT ORDER?

When teaching the consonant sounds, you do not have to present the letters in alphabetical order. Many teachers, for example, introduce the sounds of *m* and *s* first because these letters appear most frequently in English. Whatever order you choose, make sure that you do not present two letters with similar sounds one after the other, such as *b* and *d*. (Activities for the individual letters begin on page 16; these pages have been set out according to the alphabet to make it easier for you to find the pages you need.)

SOUND CHARTS *Class Activity*

As you present each consonant, have the students make a class chart that spotlights its sound. First, write the consonant on a sheet of chart paper and post it in the classroom. Then have your students complete the chart by gluing on magazine pictures or drawings of items beginning with the consonant the class is learning. Small items (such as buttons or beads for the letter *B*) can also be glued onto the chart.

Class Activity

Sharing Time

Add an extra challenge to your students' sharing time by assigning a consonant theme every so often. For example, if your class has been working with the sound of *t*, have them bring items that begin with *t* for sharing. Afterwards, display the items that were shared on a table and let the children examine the items more closely.

CONSONANT MINI-CHARTS
Class Activity

Reproduce the chart on page 15 for every student. Instruct each child to glue the chart on the front of a file folder. Have the students write their names on the folders and then let the children keep them in their desks or mailboxes as a handy reference.

As your class completes activity sheets that reinforce consonant sounds, have the children place their work in their folders. Every so often, staple the pages together for the students to take home to show their parents.

COVER THE CONSONANTS
Class Activity

Use page 15 to give a quick review of the consonants. Hand out a copy of the page and several counters to each child. Then say a word, and have the students cover the consonant they hear at the beginning of the word. Repeat the activity several times, using a different consonant each time.

BAGGED LETTERS
Class Activity

Reproduce one copy of page 15 and cut apart the consonants. Place the letters in a paper lunch bag. Then call on a student to draw a consonant out of the bag. Ask the child to name the consonant and state a word beginning with that letter. Then let that child call on another student to draw a letter. Repeat the activity several times.

Game
Pillowcase Fun

Place several items in a pillowcase. Include objects that begin with the consonant sound your class has been learning. Next, divide the students into two teams. Tell them that they will be looking for items that begin with the letter they have been studying. Then call on one child from each team to pull out an item from the pillowcase, state its name, and say the beginning sound of the word. If the item begins with the designated consonant, the child's team gets two points. If not, the team gets one point. Continue the game until all the objects have been taken out of the pillowcase. The team with the most points wins.

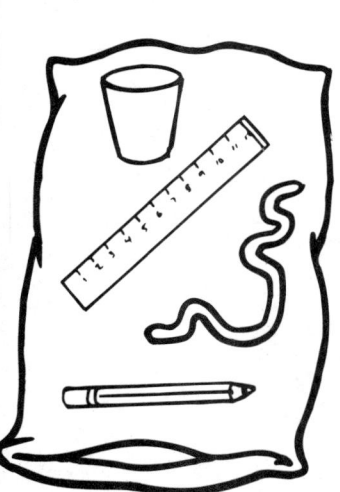

SIT OR STAND
Listening Activity

Students begin this activity by sitting down. Instruct them to listen for a specific consonant, such as *m*. Then say words one at a time. Each time the students hear a word that begins with the designated consonant, they stand up. If, while standing, they hear a word that begins with a different consonant, they sit down. Continue the activity for several minutes. As your class gains confidence in distinguishing consonants, increase the speed at which you say the words.

Name _____

A Consonant Chart

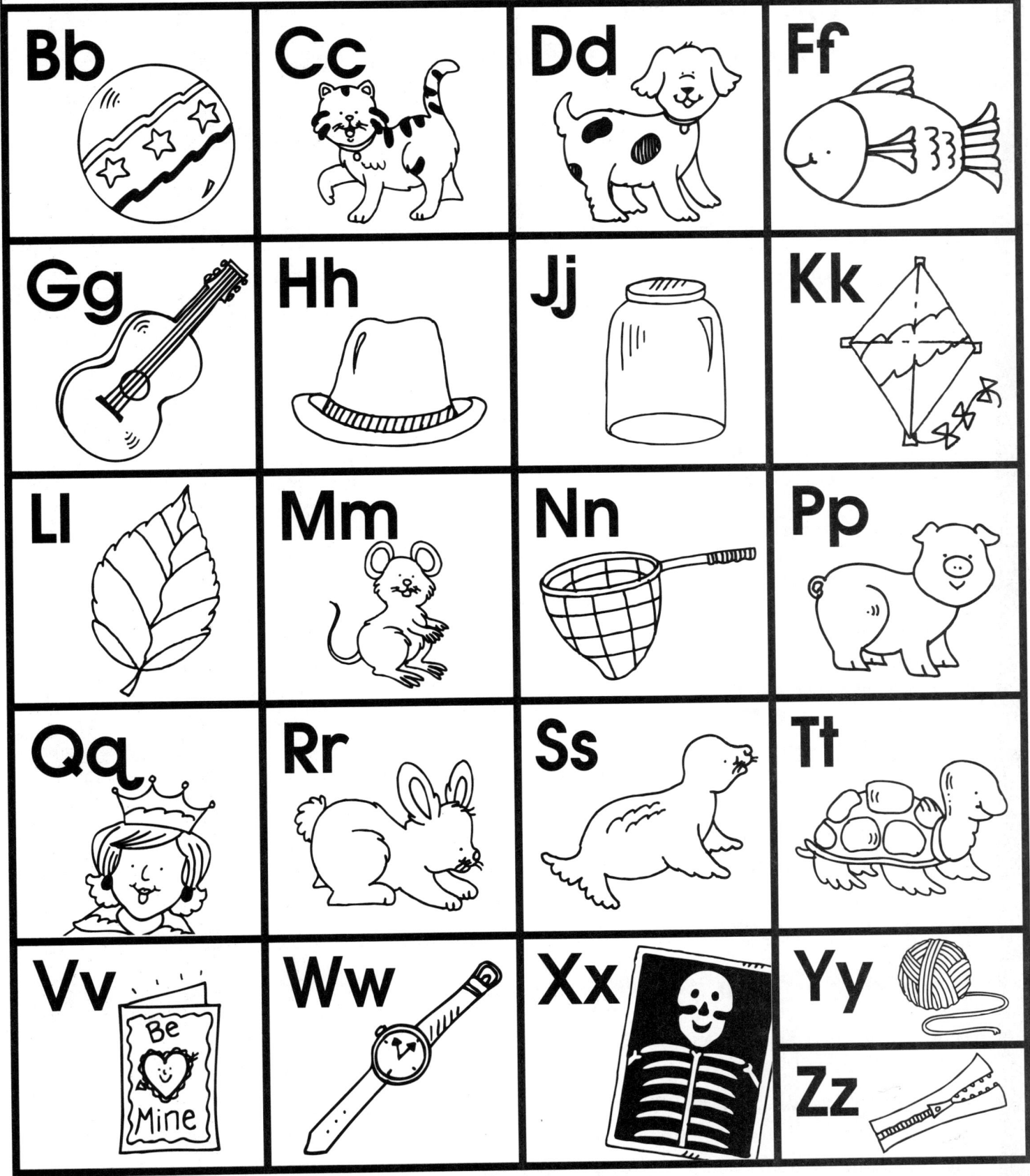

The Sound of B

WHAT'S IN THE BAG?
Class Activity

To prepare for this activity, you will need to get several small objects that begin with *b*, such as a book, a bell, a ball, a balloon, and a bottle of bubbles. Place the objects in a paper grocery bag.

Show the bag to the students and tell them that the objects that are inside have one thing in common. Then take out the items one at a time, and have the class name the objects as they appear. After the bag has been emptied, elicit from the class that the items have the same beginning sound.

Next, list the items that were in the bag on the chalkboard. Guide the students into seeing that each word begins with *b*. Then have the students read the list with you as they listen carefully to the *b* sound.

A "B" POEM
Class Activity

Write this poem on the chalkboard and read it to the class.

> Bobby bought a book.
>
> Bobby baked some bread.
>
> Bobby took a bath,
>
> Then went straight to bed!

Ask the students to point out the words in the poem that begin with *b*, and call on volunteers to circle those words. Then have the students recite the poem, and have them make up actions for each line.

A "B" BOOKLET
Class Activity

For a follow-up activity to the poem above, write the following sentence on the board: *Bobby bought big books.* Then ask the students to suggest other *b* items that Bobby could have bought, and write their suggestions below the word *books*. Next, pass out sheets of paper, and have each child illustrate one item that Bobby bought. Have the students write *Bobby bought big ____* to describe their pictures. Then staple the sheets together to make a booklet for the classroom library.

POP THE BUBBLES
Class Activity

Draw five or six "bubbles" (circles) on the board and in each one write a short word beginning with *b*, such as *bat, bed, ball,* or *bell.* If you like, add a simple picture that illustrates each word. Then ask a student volunteer to read one of the words. If the child can, then he or she can erase the circle and "pop" the bubble. Continue the activity with other students until all the bubbles have been popped.

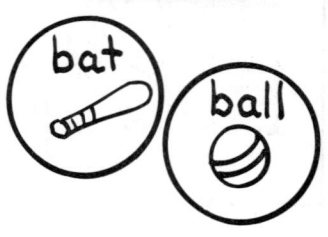

Name _____

The Sound of B

Color the pictures that begin with the sound of **b**.

 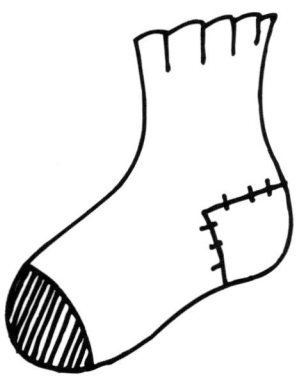

 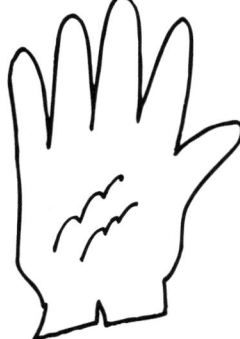 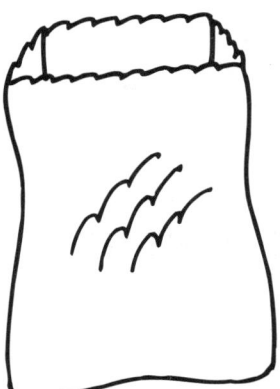

Write **Bb**.

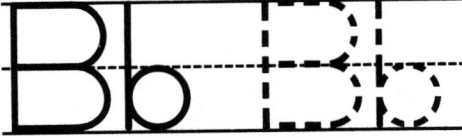

reproducible

The Sound of C

HEAR AND CLAP
Class Activity

Say several words that begin with *c*, such as *cat*, *coat*, *can*, *corn*, and *cup*. Have the class listen to the words and tell you the sound that is common to each. Write the words on the chalkboard, and have the students see that the letter *c* produces the beginning sound. Point to each word and have the class say it with you.

Next, tell the students to listen carefully as you say some more words. Instruct the children to clap as soon as they hear a word beginning with *c*. Continue the game with a variety of words to give the class ample opportunities to distinguish the *c* sound.

A "C" POEM
Class Activity

Write the following poem on a sheet of chart paper:

> A cow is crunching corn.
>
> Come and see!
>
> A cow is crunching corn
>
> Under a tree!

Read the poem to your class, pointing to the words as you say them. Call on student volunteers to underline words beginning with *c*. Then have the children recite the poem and clap out the rhythm. Ask students to make up new words for the first and third lines. (Examples: *a cat is cooking cabbage; a crocodile is crying; a crab is climbing carefully*) Add the new verses to the chart, and have the children read the poem and clap out the beat.

COLORFUL CATERPILLARS
Group Activity

Divide the class into small groups. Give each group several 4-inch circles cut from different colors of construction paper. Then tell the students that each group is to brainstorm words that begin with *c*. Instruct the children to write or illustrate the words on the circles.

Next, show the groups how to tape or glue the circles together to form a caterpillar's body. Have the students finish their caterpillars by adding a circle for the head and drawing the facial features. Afterwards, let the groups share their caterpillars and their words with the class.

Name _____

The Sound of C

Draw a line from each cat to a picture that begins with the sound of **c**.

Write **Cc**.

The Sound of D

CONSONANTS

WHAT DOESN'T BELONG?
Class Activity

Say several words that begin with *d*, such as *dog, duck,* and *doll.* Have the students tell you what sound they hear at the beginning of each word. Then write the words on the blackboard, and have the students see that the letter *d* produces the beginning sound. Next, ask the students to listen carefully as you say three words: *desk, door, clock.* Have the class pick out the word that does not have the *d* sound. Continue the activity with other groups of words. Here are some suggestions to get you started: *school, dirt, down; deer, goat, donkey; dance, run, dive; penny, dime, dollar.*

A "D" POEM
Class Activity

Write the following poem on a sheet of chart paper:

> Did dinosaurs dream,
>
> Do you think, do you think?
>
> Did dinosaurs dream,
>
> Do you think?
>
> If dinosaurs dreamed, if dinosaurs dreamed,
>
> What did they dream, do you think?

Teach the poem to your class, pointing to the words as you say them. Have individual children use a highlighter pen to circle the words that begin with *d*. Then have the children recite the poem with you. For a follow-up activity, let students draw pictures of dinosaurs dreaming. Have each student draw a large cloud above his or her dinosaur and draw a picture inside to show what the animal is dreaming about. Later, have the students copy and complete this sentence under their pictures: *This dinosaur dreamed about __.*

SPOT THE WORD
Class Activity

Say a sentence in which one word begins with *d*. Have the class pick out the *d* word. Here are some sentences you may wish to start with: *I have four dimes. Do you like carrots? It is dark at night. A duck can swim.* For an extra challenge, say sentences that have two or more words that begin with *d*, as in the following: *David likes to dance. That doll costs ten dollars. Does your dog like to dig?*

Name_____

The Sound of D

Look at each box. Color the picture that begins with the sound of **d**.

Write **Dd**.

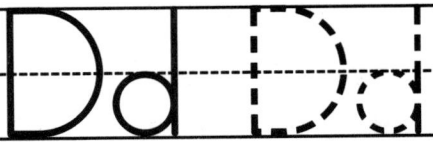

The Sound of F

CONSONANTS

OBJECTS THAT BEGIN WITH "F"

Class Activity

Bring to school a variety of objects (or pictures of objects) that begin with *f*, such as a fork, a funnel, a fan, and a feather. Have the children name the objects and guide them into seeing that the words all have the same beginning sound. List the objects on the board. Then ask the students for other words that begin with *f*, and add them to the list. Call on one student at a time to circle the *f* in each word.

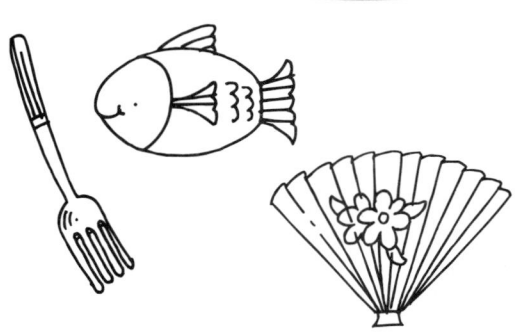

RAISE YOUR HAND

Class Activity

Tell your students to close their eyes and listen while you say some words. Tell them to raise their hands whenever they hear a word beginning with *f*. As you say the words, watch to see if the children can distinguish the *f* sound. Make a note of the ones who cannot, and then later work with those students on an individual or small-group basis.

AN "F" POEM

Class Activity

Recite the following poem to your class:

> F–f–f! (the name of the letter)
>
> I like the sound of F!
>
> Fresh fish, fresh fish,
>
> F–f–f!

Have the class say the poem with you and point out the words that have the *f* sound. Then let the children add new verses by replacing the words *fresh fish*. Here are some ideas: *furry fox, fine friends, fancy fans, five fingers*.

FOLLOW THE FOOTPRINTS

Class Activity

Cut out paper footprints, and on each one write or illustrate a word that begins with *f*. Arrange the footprints on a bulletin board or along the wall. Then challenge the class to "follow the footprints" by saying the words aloud.

FS123306 Phonics Made Simple—Kindergarten ■ © Frank Schaffer Publications, Inc.

Name ______________________________

The Sound of F

Draw a line from each fish to a picture that begins with the sound of **f**.

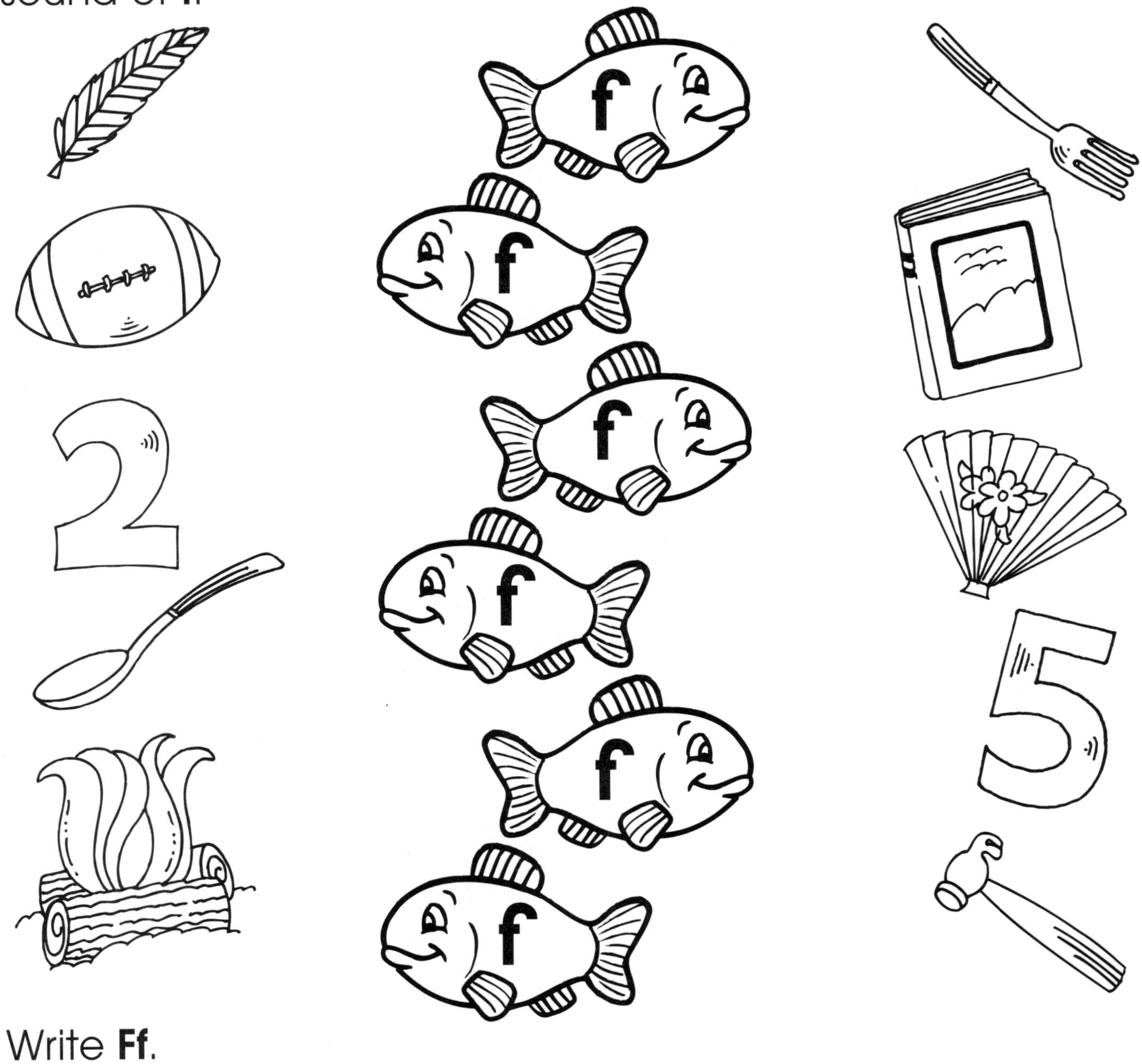

Write **Ff**.

Ff

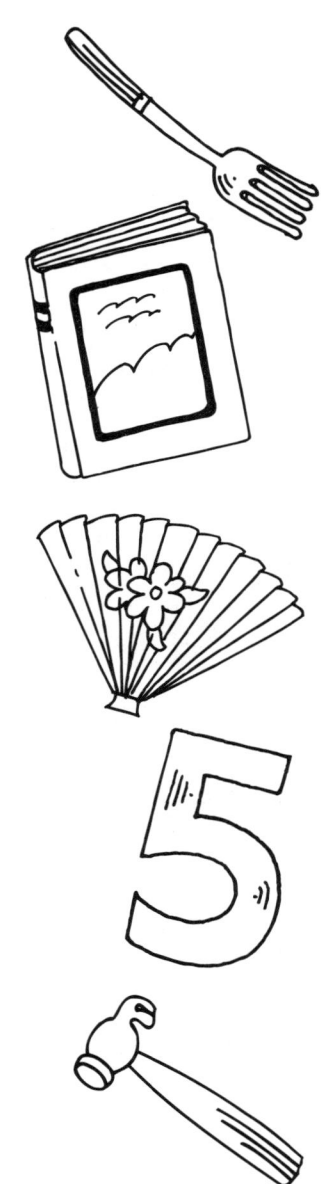

The Sound of G

MYSTERY SOUND

Class Activity

Tell the students that you are going to find out who would make good detectives in your class. Then say the following sentences, and have the children see if they can use the clues to figure out the mystery sound: *A gorilla has it but a monkey doesn't. A goose has it but a duck doesn't. A goat has it but a cow doesn't. A garden has it but a yard doesn't.* As you say each sentence, make sure that you emphasize the words that are being compared (*gorilla/monkey, goose/duck,* and so on).

After the students discover that the mystery sound is the *g* sound, write the *g* words on the board. Point to each word, and have the children read it aloud to hear the beginning sound. Then let the class suggest other words that begin with *g*, such as *gas, gum, get,* and *game*.

A "G" POEM

Class Activity

Write the following poem on the blackboard:

> Go, goat, go!
>
> Don't be slow!
>
> To the gate, don't be late!
>
> Go, goat, go!

Have the students say the poem with you, and have them point out the words that begin with a *g* sound. Then have them repeat the poem several times, substituting *goat* with other *g* words. (Examples: *goose, gorilla, gopher*)

GOOFY SENTENCES

Class Activity

Ask your class to help you write a list of "goofy sentences" that contain words beginning with *g*. Start by writing these sentences on the chalkboard: *Gorillas get grumpy. Goats grab garden hoses. Geese giggle and giggle. Gophers get gum at grocery stores.* Then have the children contribute other sentences. Afterwards, have each child select one sentence and illustrate it. Tell the students to complete their pictures by copying the corresponding sentence underneath. Have the students underline the words that begin with *g*.

Name_____

The Sound of G

Color the pictures that begin with the sound of **g**.

Write **Gg**.

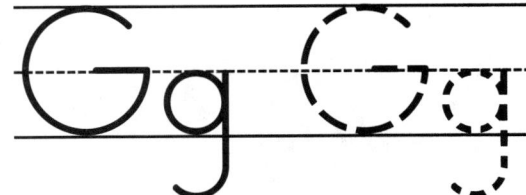

The Sound of H

AN "H" POEM

Class Activity

Teach the following poem to your class:

"Hurry!" said the hippo.

"Hurry!" said the hen.

And the two hurried up a hill,

And hurried down again.

Have the class say the poem with you. After the last line, have the students huff—*Huh, huh, huh*— as if they were tired. Tell the students that the huffing sound is like the sound that the *h* makes. Then have the students point out the *h* words in the poem.

PARTS-OF-THE-BODY RIDDLES

Class Activity

Challenge the class to guess the answers to the following riddles. Tell the students that each answer names a part of the body and begins with *h*:

You write with this. (hand)

This is attached to your neck. (head)

This is cut every so often. (hair)

This is just below your waist. (hip)

This is on the back of your foot. (heel)

This pumps blood through your body. (heart)

HANGING WORDS

Group Activity

Divide the class into small groups, and give each group several index cards. Instruct each group to write or illustrate an *h* word on each card. Then have the group members tape the cards to a length of yarn so that the words hang. Let the groups share their words with the class. Afterwards, hang the words on a bulletin board or along the chalkboard ledge.

Name _____

The Sound of H

Look at each space in the puzzle. If it has a picture that begins with the sound of **h**, color the space red. If it does not, color the space blue.

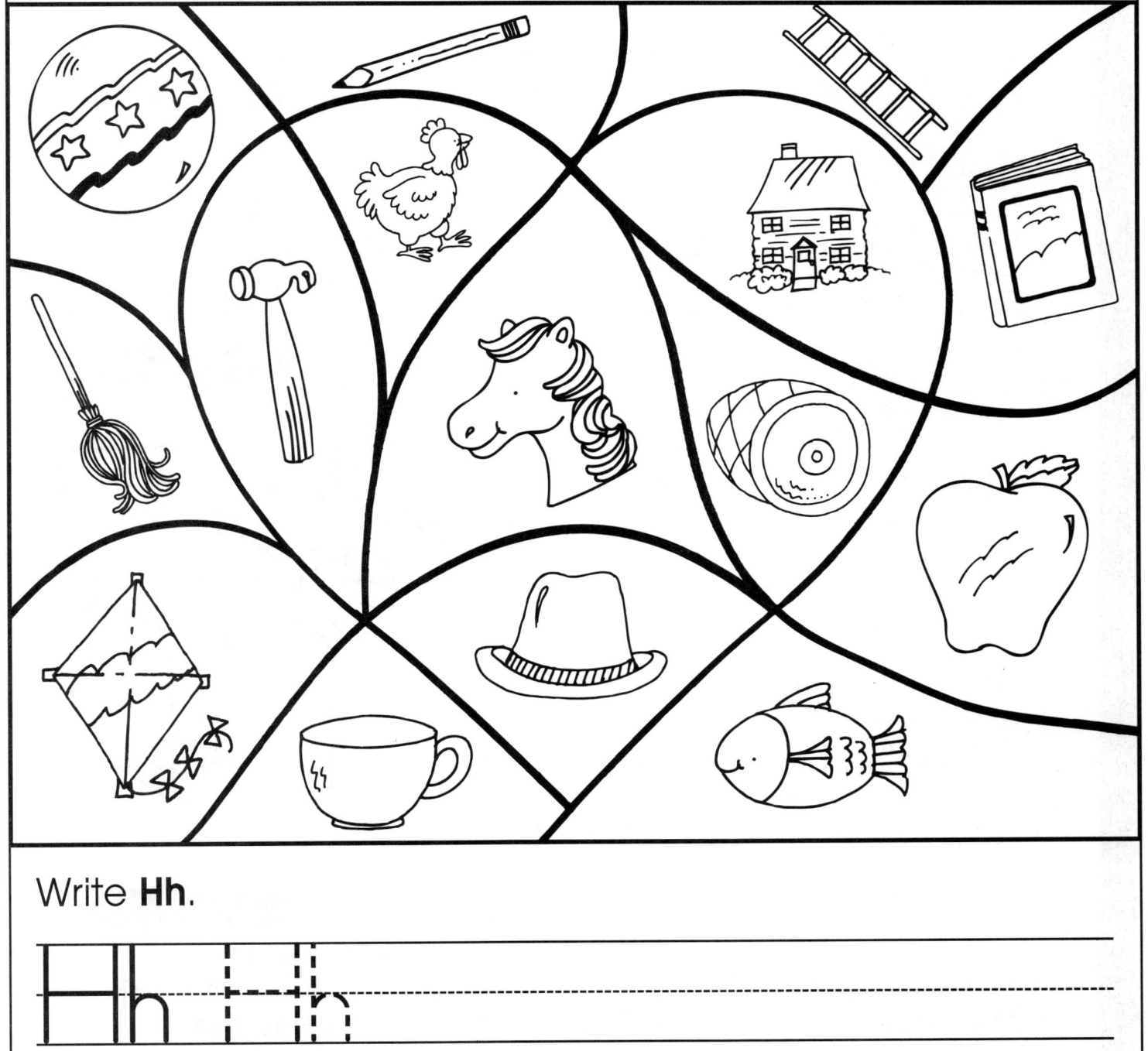

Write **Hh**.

The Sound of J

JOLLY JO-JO
Class Activity

Bring a clown puppet or doll to the class. (If you do not have one, draw a picture of a clown.) Introduce the clown to the students as Jolly Jo-Jo. Explain that Jolly Jo-Jo's name begins with *j*. Then have the students say the name to get the feel of the *j* sound.

Next, tell the class that Jolly Jo-Jo only likes things that begin with *j*. Then have the students listen to the following questions and give you the answer:

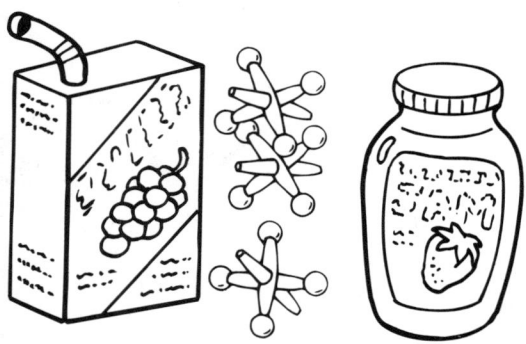

Does Jolly Jo-Jo like juice or milk?

Does Jolly Jo-Jo like butter or jam on her crackers?

Does Jolly Jo-Jo like to play jacks or marbles?

Does Jolly Jo-Jo drive a truck or a jeep?

Does Jolly Jo-Jo like to jog or ride a bike?

Does Jolly Jo-Jo like to travel by boat or by jet?

A "J" POEM
Class Activity

Teach your class this poem about a jack-in-the-box:

> Down in his little box,
>
> The jumping jack lies low.
>
> Then suddenly up he jumps,
>
> Hello, Jack, hello!

Have the students say the poem with you and name the words that begin with *j*. Then tell the students to crouch on the floor and pretend that each one is a jack-in-the-box. Instruct the class to listen as you say some words. When the students hear you say a word beginning with *j*, they are to jump up and call out hello. Repeat the activity several times.

A "J" SNACK
Class Activity

After your students have had a chance to work with the sound of *j* for a few days, celebrate their learning by treating the class to a special snack. Bring items that include words that begin with *j*. For example, juice in a jug, crackers with jam, or a jar of jelly beans make yummy treats your class is sure to enjoy!

The Sound of J

Look at the jugglers and their balls. Color the balls that have pictures of things that begin with the sound of **j**.

Write **Jj**.

The Sound of K

SOUND TWINS
Class Activity

Show pictures of a key, a kitten, a kite, and a kangaroo to your class. Have the students name the pictures and tell you the sound they hear at the beginning of the words. Write the words on the board, and have the class notice that each one begins with *k*. Some children may notice that the beginning sound is the same sound produced by *c*. Tell the class that *c* and *k* can produce the same sound; add that some names, such as Cathy/Kathy and Chris/Kris, can be spelled with either letter. Explain that as the children work more and more with the words, they will learn to remember which words begin with *c* and which ones begin with *k*.

RHYME TIME
Class Activity

Tell your students that you will say a word and that they will have to figure out a word that rhymes and begins with *k*. Then say the word *ring*; the class will respond with *king*. Continue the activity with other rhyming clues, such as *bite (kite), sick (kick), miss (kiss), fit (kit), lid (kid),* and *mitten (kitten).*

A "K" POEM
Class Activity

Write the following poem on the chalkboard.

> Do kings go to the kitchen
>
> And wash dishes in the sink?
>
> Do they empty out the kettle?
>
> Is that kinglike, do you think?

Have the class say the poem with you. Call on student volunteers to underline the words that begin with *k*. Then have the children replace the third line with other sentences that use words beginning with *k*. (Examples: *Do they wash out ketchup bottles? Do they fly kites in the sky? Do they look for hungry kittens?*)

Name _____

The Sound of K

Color the pictures that begin with the sound of **k**.

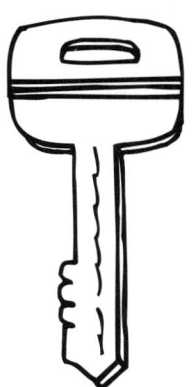
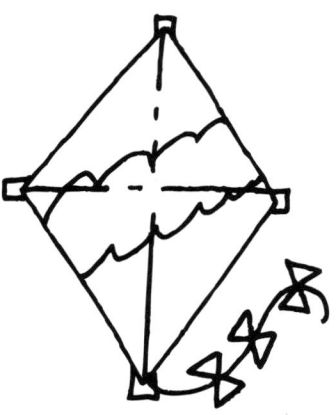

Write **Kk**.

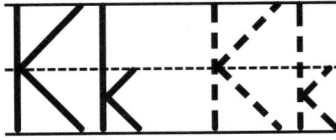

The Sound of L

LULU'S PICTURES
Class Activity

Bring a doll to school and introduce her to the class as Lulu. Tell the class that Lulu loves drawing. Then tell the students to listen as you tell them what Lulu likes to draw:

Lulu likes to draw lemons and limes.

Lulu loves to draw ladybugs and lizards.

Lulu is learning to draw lions and lambs.

Lulu is learning to draw lilies and lilacs.

Ask the students what kinds of pictures Lulu likes to draw, and elicit from them the fact that each of the things Lulu draws begins with *l*. Then have the class name other things that Lulu might like to draw (examples: leaves, logs, lines, landscapes, lobsters).

AN "L" POEM
Class Activity

Teach the class the following poem:

Look at the lion leap!

Look at the lion land!

Look at the lion limp!

Please lend the lion a hand!

Have the students say the *l* words that are in the poem. Then have the students say the poem and do the accompanying actions:

leap—stand with arms outstretched

land—crouch on the floor

limp—hobble in place

CLIMB THE LADDER
Class Activity

Draw a large ladder on a sheet of chart paper. On each rung, tape a flashcard that has a word or picture of something that begins with *l* (examples: log, leaf, lamp, line, lion). Then have the students help you "climb" the ladder by saying each of the *l* words, beginning with the word on the bottom rung.

Name _____

The Sound of L

Look at the living room. Draw a circle around five things that begin with the sound of **l**. Color the picture.

Write **Ll**.

_____

The Sound of M

LISTEN FOR THE SOUND
Class Activity

Tell the students to close their eyes. Explain that you are going to say some words. Tell the children that as soon as they think they know what sound is common to each word, they are to raise their hands while still keeping their eyes shut. Then have the class listen as you say these words: *mat, milk, mug, moon, mom, mop*. Watch to see how long it takes the children to figure out the common sound.

Next, ask the students to open their eyes. List the words on the chalkboard. Have the children notice that the letter *m* produces the beginning sound of each word. Point to the words on the list and have the class say the words with you.

GOING TO THE MARKET
Class Activity

Tell the class that you are going to the market and that you are going to buy items that begin with *m*. Then give the following clues and challenge your students to guess what you are going to buy:

This is something to drink. (milk)

This can be made into hamburger. (meat)

This is yellow and it tastes good on toast. (margarine)

This is white and it is spread on sandwiches. (mayonnaise)

This is yellow and spicy. It can be spread on hot dogs. (mustard)

This grows on the ground. It looks like a small umbrella. (mushroom)

These are candies that taste good after a meal. (mints)

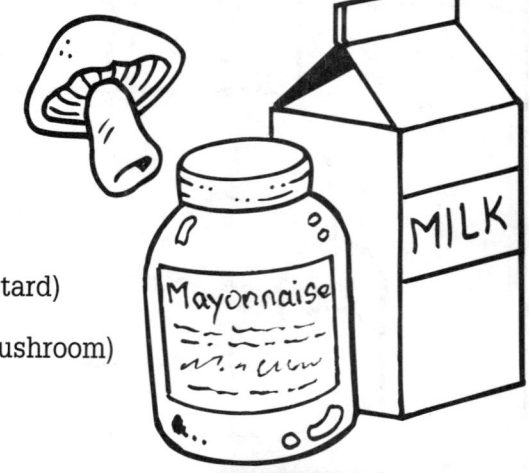

AN "M" POEM
Class Activity

Teach students the following poem:

Milk is yummy! M-m-m!

It's good in my tummy! M-m-m!

Melons are yummy! M-m-m!

They're good in my tummy! M-m-m!

Let the students say the poem and clap out the rhythm, and have them exaggerate the *m* sound at the end of each line. Then ask the class to make up new lines with other foods that begin with *m*.

Name _____

The Sound of M

Draw a line from each mouse to a picture that begins with the sound of **m**.

Write **Mm**.

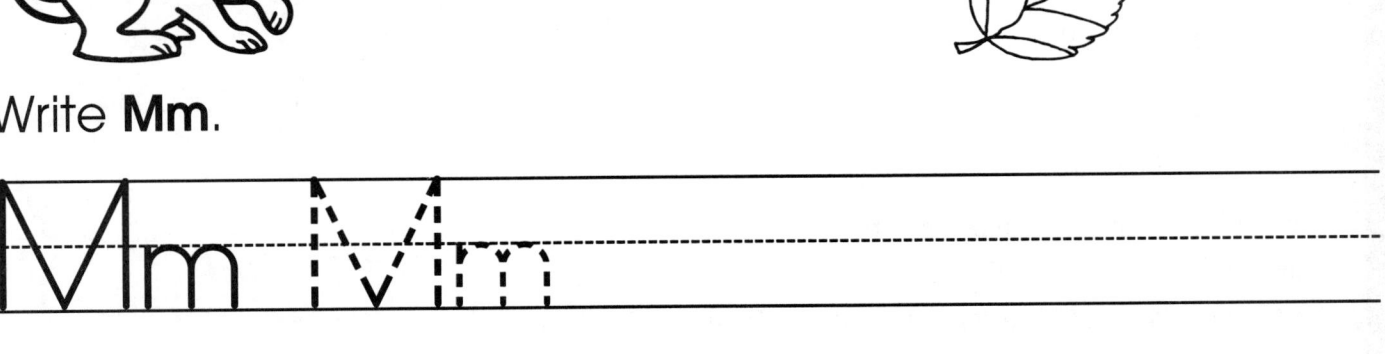

The Sound of N

AN "N" SCAVENGER HUNT
Class Activity

Collect several items that begin with *n*, such as a nail, a nut, a needle, a nickel, a napkin, a necklace, and a net. List the items on a sheet of paper. Next, hide the objects around the classroom before the students arrive. Later, tell the students that they are going on a scavenger hunt in the classroom. Explain that they are going to find a special group of items. Then read the list to the class. Ask what the objects have in common, and elicit the fact that each item begins with the *n* sound. List the items on the chalkboard, and include a simple drawing beside each one. Have the class see that the letter *n* produces the beginning sound. Then instruct the students to quietly move around the room in search of the objects listed on the board. As each item is found, check it off on the list. Keep playing the game until all the items have been found.

I WENT EXPLORING
Class Activity

Here's a memory game that lets students practice saying the *n* sound. First, collect six or seven pictures of objects that begin with *n* (see the list above). Glue each picture onto a sheet of construction paper, and label each item. Place the papers along the chalkboard ledge, with the pictures facing the board.

Next, tell the students that they are going to play an "Exploring Game." Have the children imagine that they are exploring and looking for *n* words. Then call on one student to turn over the first picture. As the child turns the picture over, he or she says *I went exploring and found a _____* , completing the sentence with the name of the picture. Call on another child to turn over the second picture. As the child does this, he or she says *I went exploring and found a _____ and a _____* , naming the first two pictures. Call on a third child to turn over the third picture on the ledge. This child says *I went exploring and found a _____ , a _____ , and a _____*, naming the three pictures that are turned over. Continue the game until all the pictures have been turned over. If you like, change the order of the pictures and play the game with the class again.

AN "N" POEM
Class Activity

Teach students the following poem:

>Norman nibbles nuts,
>
>Nine nuts a day,
>
>Especially at nighttime,
>
>He nibbles away!

Have the students say the poem with you. Then have the students make up new versions of the poem. (Example: Norman naps a lot/Nine times a day/Especially at nighttime/He naps away!)

Name _____

The Sound of N

Color each egg that has a picture of something that begins with the sound of **n**.

Write **Nn**.

The Sound of P

WHAT'S IN THE PURSE?
Class Activity

Get a large purse and place inside it items that begin with *p*, such as a pencil, a paintbrush, a peanut, a pear, and a puppet. Then show the purse to the students and call on one child at a time to take out an item. As the object is revealed, have the student say its name and lay it on a table. When the purse has been emptied, point to each item and have the class say its name. Guide the class into seeing that the items begin with the same beginning sound. List the items on the board, and have them see that the letter *p* makes the beginning sound.

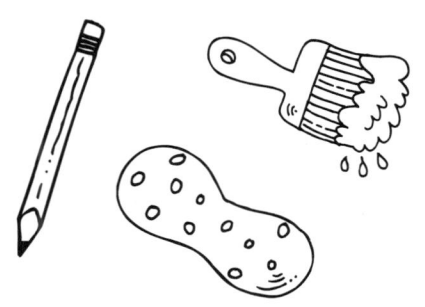

A "P" POEM
Class Activity

Your students will enjoy practicing the *p* sound with this fun poem:

> The popcorn's popping.
>
> It's popping in the pot.
>
> Poppity pop! Poppity pop!
>
> It's piping hot!

Have the students recite the poem three times, and challenge them to say the words faster and faster after each time.

A "P" PIE
Group Activity

Divide the class into small groups, and give each group grocery store flyers and an aluminum pie pan. Tell the students that they are going to make *p* pies—pies that are made up of ingredients that begin with the sound of *p*. Then instruct each group to cut out items from the flyers that begin with *p* and put the pictures in the pie pan (examples: peanuts, popcorn, peach, pear, pineapple, pumpkin, pepperoni, plum, potato, pepper, peas, parsley). Afterwards, have the groups glue their pictures onto a large paper circle representing a pie. Let the students share their pies with the class and have them name each ingredient they chose.

Name _____

The Sound of P

Draw a circle around six things that begin with the sound of **p**. Color the picture.

Write **Pp**.

The Sound of Q

A WORD QUILT

Class Activity

Say these words to the class: *quack, quilt, queen, quit, quiz, quick, quiet, quill, quarter*. Ask the students what sound they hear at the beginning of the words. (Some children might respond that they hear a *c* or a *k*. This is a reasonable guess, since the sounds are so similar.) Then have the class watch as you write the words on a special "word quilt." On the chalkboard draw a quilt made up of a 3 x 3 grid. Inside the grid write the nine words. Include picture clues beside some of the words, such as a picture of a queen or a quarter. Then tell the class to listen as you point to the words and read them. Guide the students into seeing that each word begins with *qu*. Explain that in the English language the letter *q* is always followed by the letter *u*.

A HAPPY FACE GAME

Class Activity

Give each student a three-inch paper square and a craft stick. Have the students draw a happy face on the square and then glue it onto the stick. Tell the students to listen as you say some words. Instruct them to hold up their happy faces whenever they hear a word beginning with *q*. Then say several *q* words to the class, inserting other words between them. To avoid confusion, do not include words that begin with *c* or *k*.

A "Q" POEM

Write the following poem on the chalkboard:

> A queen made a quilt,
>
> A quilter was she.
>
> And when she made a quilt,
>
> She quilted quietly.

Ask student volunteers to underline the words that begin with *q*. Then have the class recite the poem three times, saying the words more quietly each time.

Name _____

The Sound of Q

Color the spaces yellow if they have pictures that begin with the sound of **q**. Color the other spaces orange.

Write **Qq**.

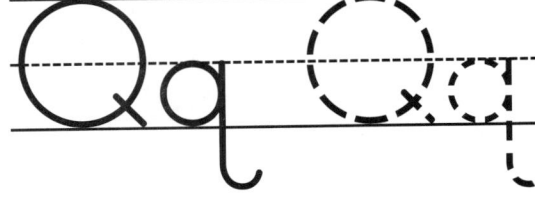

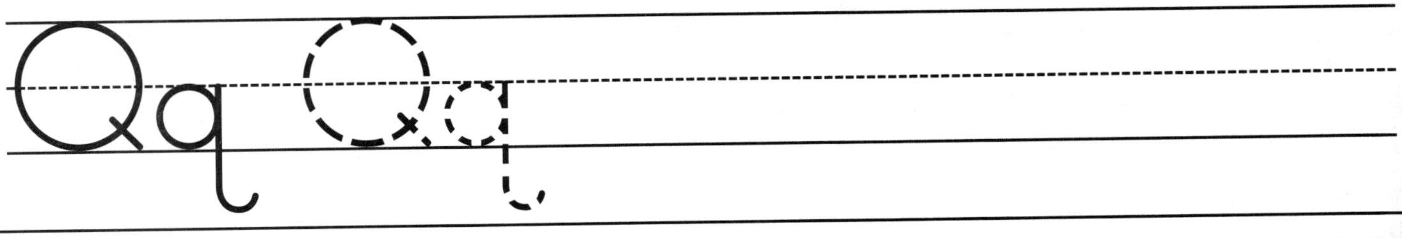

reproducible 41

FS123306 Phonics Made Simple—Kindergarten ■ © Frank Schaffer Publications, Inc.

The Sound of R

CONSONANTS

PICTURE THIS

Class Activity

Tell the students to close their eyes and listen as you say the following phrases: *red rose, rocky road, round rug, rusty rake, rubber raft, racing rabbits.* As you say each phrase, have the students imagine a picture of what you are describing. Ask the children what they notice about the sound of the words. Guide them into seeing that each word begins with an *r* sound. Write the words on the chalkboard and have the class notice the *r* in front of each word. Call on students to underline the letter that makes the beginning sound of each word.

AN "R" POEM

Class Activity

Write the following poem on a sheet of chart paper:

> Run, rabbit, run!
>
> Running is such fun!
>
> Then rest inside your little home
>
> After you are done.

Have students point out the words that begin with *r*. Then have them say the poem with you. Afterwards, have them recite other versions of the poem by replacing the word *run* with *race, rake,* and *read.*

AN "R" RELAY

Class Activity

Divide the class into teams. For each team, prepare a box of items or pictures that represent words beginning with *r*. For example, you could include the following items: ribbon, rope, ring, rose, rock, rice, and ruler. Place the boxes several feet away from the teams.

Next, call out a word naming something in the box. Have the first student in each team run to his or her team's box, find the item, and run back. Call out another word, and have the second student run and look for the item. Continue until all the students have had a chance to run.

FS123306 Phonics Made Simple—Kindergarten • © Frank Schaffer Publications, Inc.

Name _____

The Sound of R

Draw a line from each rabbit to a picture that begins with the sound of **r**.

Write **Rr**.

The Sound of S

WHAT'S IN MY SUITCASE?

Class Activity

Fill a small suitcase with items beginning with *s*, such as a pair of socks, a pair of scissors, a bar of soap, a scarf, a postage stamp, a can of soup, and a salt shaker. Then bring the suitcase to school, and show it to the class. Take out one item at a time, and have the class name it. When all the items have been taken out, ask the students what they have in common. (The words begin with *s*.) List the items on the chalkboard, and have the students notice that the letter *s* makes the beginning sound.

"S" RIDDLES

Class Activity

Make picture cards of the following words: *sun, sock, scissors, sack, six, seven, soap, stop sign, sailboat, saw*. Include both the picture and the word. Then display the cards on a chalkboard ledge. Have the class guess the words as you give these clues:

You use this to cut paper. (scissors)   This warns you to stop. (stop sign)

You use this to cut wood. (saw)   This takes you across the water. (sailboat)

This number comes after 5. (six)   You wear this on your foot. (sock)

This number comes before 8. (seven)   This shines in the sky. (sun)

Whenever a word is guessed correctly, have a student turn that card over on the ledge.

AN "S" SONG

Class Activity

Teach students this version of the traditional song "A Sailor Went to Sea":

> A sailor went to sea, sea, sea,
>
> To see what he could see, see, see,
>
> And all that he could see, see, see,
>
> Was a sea horse swimming in the sea, sea, sea.

Have the students sing the song and point out the words that begin with *s*. Then have the class make up other versions of the song by replacing *sea horse swimming* with new phrases. (Examples: *seal singing, sandwich soaking, surfer surfing, sailboat sailing*) Later, have the class draw pictures illustrating the phrases.

Name _____

The Sound of S

Draw a circle around seven things that begin with the sound of **s**. Color the picture.

Write **Ss**.

Ss Ss

The Sound of T

TERRIFIC SENTENCES
Class Activity

Tell the students to listen to the following sentences and tell you what is so "terrific" about them:

Terry talked to Ted.

Two tigers tasted tomatoes.

Tammy turned ten today.

Elicit from the class the fact that each of the words begin with the same sound. Then write the sentences on the chalkboard. Have the students see that the letter *t* makes the beginning sounds. Challenge the students to see how many new sentences they can make by replacing any of the words. Write their sentences on the board as they dictate them to you.

WORD CHALLENGE
Class Activity

Get several index cards and make picture cards of the following words: *tent, toothbrush, turtle, turkey, tulip, toucan, teapot, tomato, toaster, ten, two, top* (a toy), and *tail*. Include both the picture and word on each card. Place the cards in a paper lunch bag. Then call on a student to draw a card from the bag, look at the word, and give clues about the picture. Challenge the rest of the class to guess the word. The student who guesses the word gets to draw the next card from the bag. Continue the game until all the words have been guessed.

A "T" POEM
Class Activity

Teach students the poem below, and have them point out the *t* words. Then have them recite the poem and do the accompanying actions.

Tiptoe, tiptoe,

Around you go,   (children tiptoe around the classroom)

Go real fast,   (children tiptoe in place fast)

Go real slow,   (children tiptoe in place slowly)

Tiptoe, tiptoe,

Turn around,   (children tiptoe in place, turning around)

Bend your knees,

And touch the ground. (children bend knees and touch the ground)

Name _____

The Sound of T

Find something that begins with **t**. Look at each space in the puzzle. If it has a picture that begins with **t**, color the space brown. If it does not, color the space green.

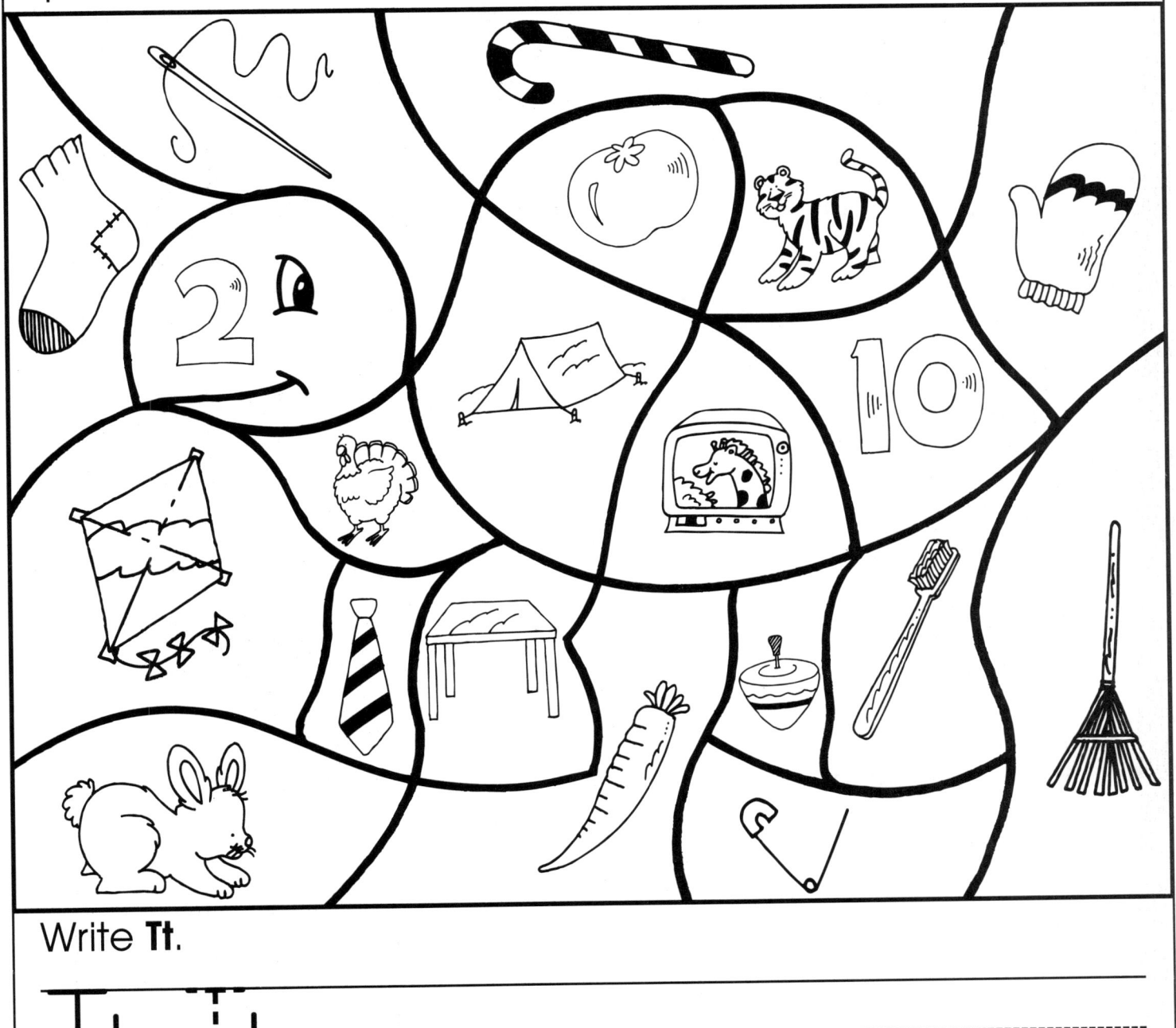

Write **Tt**.

The Sound of V

VALENTINE MAIL
Class Activity

Cut out six paper hearts and on each one write a word that begins with *v*, such as *vase, vest, vine, van, very,* and *visit*. Then fold the hearts in half and place them in a shoebox or a facial tissue box that has been covered with red paper.

Show the box to the students, and tell them that you have received some special "valentine mail." Then call on one child at a time to draw a paper heart out of the box. Have the student unfold the paper and hand it to you so that you can read the word aloud. When all the words have been read, ask the students what is common to all the valentines. Elicit from the class the fact that the words have the same beginning sound. Post the valentines on a bulletin board so that the children can see that the words begin with *v*.

Next, brainstorm with the students a list of other words that begin with *v* (examples: *vacuum, valentine, voice, volcano, vinegar, violin*). Write the children's suggestions on the board. Have student volunteers write the words on paper hearts, and display them with the other hearts. Title the bulletin board *"V" Valentines*.

LISTEN FOR THE PAIRS
Class Activity

Say three words at a time and have the class find the two words that begin with *v*. For example:

> vase, cap, vest
>
> van, volcano, hill
>
> nail, voice, vinegar

Continue the procedure with several groups of words, each time saying two words that begin with *v* and one word that does not.

A "V" POEM
Class Activity

Let students practice making the *v* sound by teaching them the following poem:

> A visitor visited me,
>
> And gave me a valentine treat
>
> With violets and lace
>
> All over the place.
>
> Wasn't that visitor sweet?

Ask students to say the words beginning with *v*, and have them notice how their lips seem to vibrate as they make the *v* sound. Then have the students recite the poem with you. For a follow-up activity, have the children draw a picture of what the valentine treat might have looked like.

Name _____

The Sound of V

Color the pictures that begin with the sound of **v**.

Write **Vv**.

The Sound of W

DO WHAT I DO   *Class Activity*

Have the students stand beside their desks. Tell them to listen to your directions and do what you do. Then say the following and do the accompanying actions:

Walk. (walk in place)

Wink. (wink to the class)

Wave. (wave to the students)

Wiggle. (wiggle in place)

After the students have copied your actions, ask them to repeat your commands. Write the words on the board, and have the children notice that the words have the same beginning sound. Call on students to underline the first letter in each word. Have the class notice that *w* makes the beginning sound.

A "W" POEM   *Class Activity*

Let students practice saying the *w* sound by teaching them this poem:

A wee worm wiggled and wiggled all day.

He wiggled at work and he wiggled at play.

He wiggled to the left.

He wiggled to the right.

He wiggled and he wiggled both day and night!

Have students stand and wiggle as they recite the poem.

WINDOW PANE WORDS   *Class Activity*

Draw a large window on a sheet of chart paper. Add curtains on the sides. Then make window panes by dividing the window into 12 sections. Have the students name words that begin with *w* (examples: *watch, window, worm, work, walk, wallet, wagon, web, water, watermelon, wish, we, wave*). Write their suggestions on the panes. Ask student volunteers to add pictures beside the words. Then post the chart in the classroom as a handy reference for the students.

Name _____

The Sound of W

Draw a line from each worm to a picture that begins with the sound of **w**.

Write **Ww**.

W w w w

The Sound of X

NOT TOO MANY WORDS

Class Activity

Have students flip through the *x* words in a dictionary or an encyclopedia. Let them see that there are very few words in English that begin with *x*. Then tell the class that sometimes the *x* at the beginning of a word sounds like the letter's name, as in *x-ray*. Explain that at other times, the *x* makes a *z* sound, as in *xylophone*. Tell students that when they hear an *x* sound at the beginning of familiar words, such as in *exciting*, the sound is made by the *e* and the *x*. Then have them listen to the *x* sound in these words: *excite, example, exam, extra, exercise*.

SPOT THE "X" SOUND

Class Activity

To give students practice in distinguishing the *x* sound, have them listen as you say several words beginning or ending with that sound (examples: *extra, box, exciting, fix, ax, six, exam*). Have the children tell you whether they hear the *x* at the beginning or the end of the word.

Afterwards, say three words at a time and have the class pick out the word that has the *x* sound (examples: *bird, box, bell*).

AN "X" POEM

Class Activity

Here's a fun poem that lets children practice saying the *x* sound:

> X, x, x!
>
> It's fun to say X!
>
> It's exercise for the mouth,
>
> X, x, x!

Let the students say the poem and clap out the rhythm. Next, challenge students to think of different ways the letter *x* can be formed with the body (examples: cross arms, cross fingers, cross legs). Then have the children repeat the poem, but this time have them beat out the rhythm by crossing their hands, arms, or legs and tapping them together.

Name_____

The Sound of X

Look for the letter **x** in the picture. There are six that you will find. Color them red. Then color the rest of the picture.

Write **Xx**. _____

The Sound of Y

CONSONANTS

LISTEN FOR THE "Y" SOUND
Class Activity

Have students listen as you say these words: *yes, you, yard, yellow, yell.* Ask the class what the words have in common. (They have the same beginning sound.) Then write the words on the board. Have students point out that the letter *y* makes the beginning sound. Next, say a word at a time and have the children listen for the *y* sound. If they hear *y*, they are to say *yes*. If not, they are to say *no*. Here are some words you might start with: *yarn, book, year, young, can, ladder, yak, table, your, yogurt.*

"Y" RIDDLES
Class Activity

Make picture cards of these words: *yellow, yak, yo-yo, yolk, yam, yarn, yawn, yard.* Include both the picture and the word on each card. Place the cards along a chalkboard ledge. Then have the class listen to your clues and guess the *y* word:

This is a color. (yellow)

This is an animal that has horns and long hair. (yak)

This is a round toy that hangs on a string. (yo-yo)

This is the yellow part of an egg. (yolk)

This is a type of sweet potato. (yam)

This is used to knit blankets and clothes. (yarn)

This is something you do when you're tired. (yawn)

This is a large piece of ground that goes around a home or a school. (yard)

Later, give each student a sheet of drawing paper. Show the children how to fold their papers into fourths to make eight-page booklets. Then have the students make vocabulary booklets of *y* words by writing the eight words in the booklet and illustrating each one.

A "Y" POEM
Class Activity

Teach students the following poem:

Do yaks eat yams with toast and jam?

Or do they prefer yams with ham?

Have the students recite the poem and point out the words that begin with *y*. Then have them make up new versions of the poem by replacing *yams* with *yogurt* and *yolks*. For a follow-up activity, have each student illustrate a line from the poem.

Name _____

The Sound of Y

Look at each picture. If it begins with **y**, circle **yes**. If it does not, circle **no**.

   yes   no      yes   no

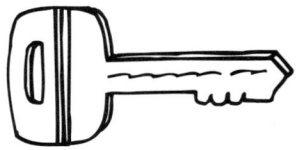   yes   no      yes   no

   yes   no      yes   no

   yes   no      yes   no

Write **Yy**.

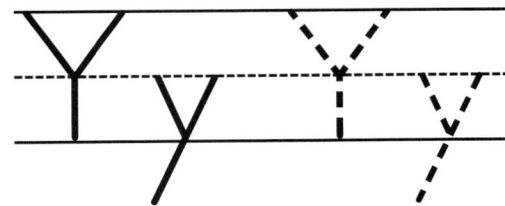

reproducible

The Sound of Z

MOSQUITO SOUNDS
Class Activity

Ask students if they have ever been near a mosquito. Tell them that a mosquito makes a loud sound as it flies—*zzzzzz!* Then have each child hold up his or her index finger and pretend it is a mosquito. Have the students move their "mosquitoes" through the air, making a *z* sound.

Tell the class that the *z* sound is produced by the letter *z*. Then have the students listen for the *z* sound as you say these words: *zero, zoo, zipper, zoom, zebra*. Ask where the *z* sound occurs (at the beginning of each word). Then write the words on the board, and have the students read the words with you. Let them emphasize the *z* sound in each word.

A ZIGZAG CHALLENGE
Class Activity

Make a zigzag path on the chalkboard. Wherever the path comes to a point, write a word beginning with *z*. Add picture clues if you like. Next, tell students that they are going to travel the zigzag path by following your finger. Then move your finger along the path, stopping at the *z* words along the way. Whenever you stop, the children must read the word your finger is pointing to.

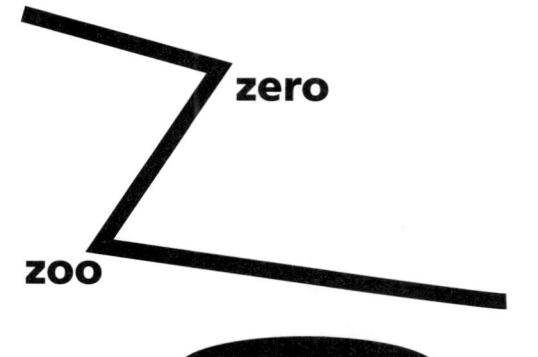

A "Z" POEM
Class Activity

Write the following poem on the chalkboard:

> A zebra zigzagged all around,
>
> All around the zoo.
>
> A zebra zigzagged all around.
>
> She zigzagged. Can you?

Have the class point out the words that begin with *z*. Then have the students say the poem with you. Next, have them repeat the poem, but this time let them zigzag around the room as they say the words. As the children say the last line, let them change *Can you?* to *I can, too!*

Name _____

The Sound of Z

Color the pictures that begin with the sound of **z**.

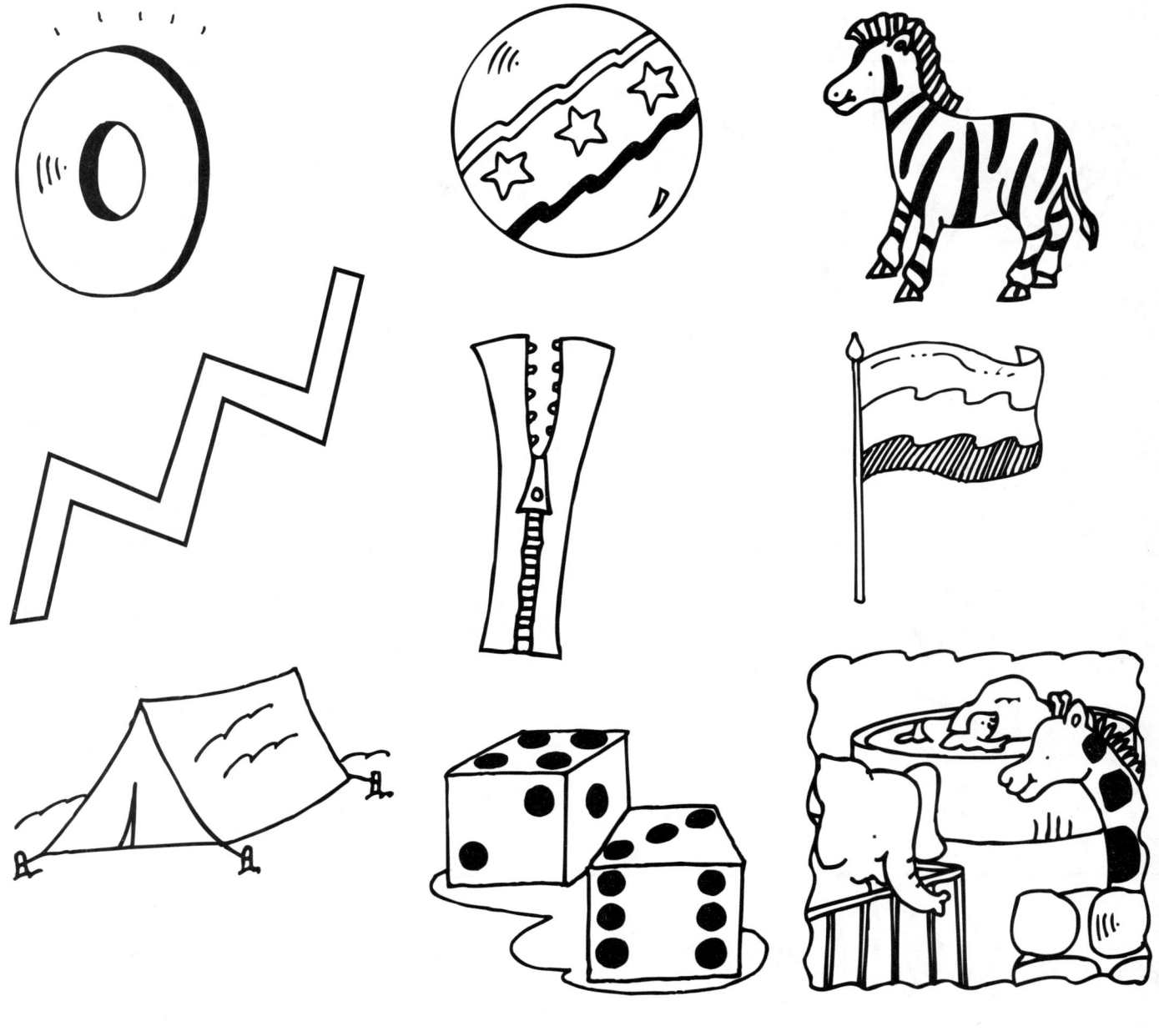

Write **Zz**.

Name _____

All Kinds of Animals

Look at each animal. Say its name. Circle the sound you hear at the beginning of the word.

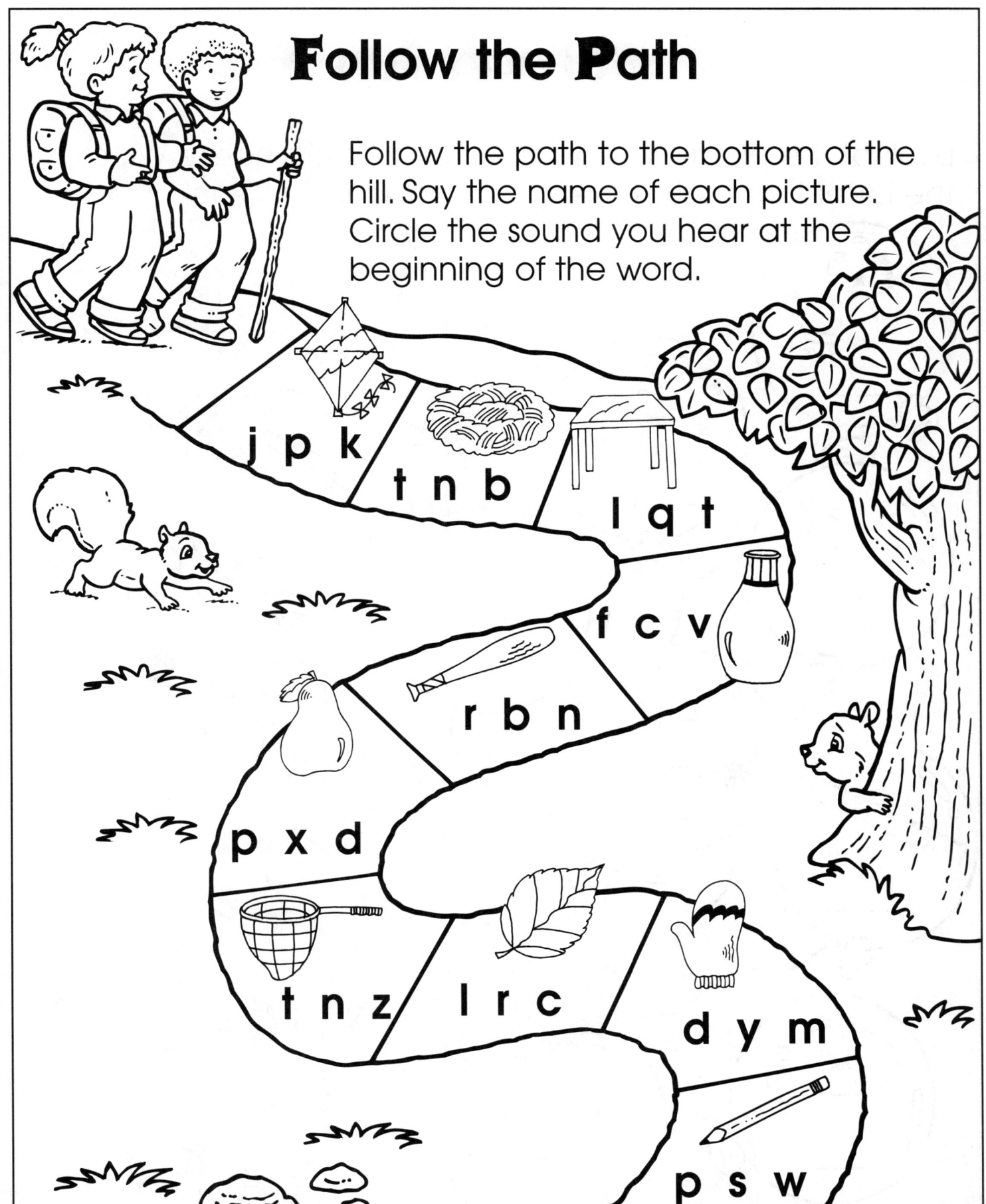

Balloon Fun

Look at the picture on each balloon. Say its name. Write the letter that makes the beginning sound of each word.

INTRODUCING FINAL CONSONANTS

As your kindergartners gain skill discriminating beginning consonants, you may want to introduce them to final consonants. (In kindergarten, final consonants should only be introduced if the children are ready.) The ideas on this page and the activity sheets on pages 62–63 will give students practice identifying ending sounds. Page 64 is a review of beginning and final consonants.

LISTEN TO THE ENDINGS *Class Activity*

Say these words to the class: *cat, pet, sit, hot*. Ask the students what the words have in common. Guide them into seeing that the words have the same ending sound. Then write the words on the chalkboard. Ask student volunteers to circle the last letter of each word. Have them see that the words all end in *t*. Then ask the students to name other words that end in *t*.

Repeat the activity at different times with other groups of words that end in the same consonant.

MATCH THE ENDING SOUNDS *Class Activity*

Tell the class that you are going to say words in groups of three. After you say each group of words, have the children point out the two words that end in the same consonant. For example, if you say *pen, rug*, and *big*, the children should notice that *rug* and *big* have the same ending sound. Here are some words you can begin with:

sit, hat, van   bell, hill, rock

leaf, web, bib   dress, stop, glass

cup, sun, hop   bread, ham, jam

Guess the Picture *Group Activity*

Prepare three or four flashcards from 3" x 9" pieces of construction paper in the following manner. Fold the paper so that the two ends meet in the center. Write the beginning and final consonants of a three-letter word on the front of the flashcard. Open the card and draw a picture of the word inside; label the picture as well. Here are some words you might use: *sun, bug, hat, cap, cup, bed*.

Close the cards. Then show them one at a time to the class. Have the students look at the consonant clues, and challenge them to guess the picture inside. When the word is guessed correctly, open the card to reveal the picture. Continue the activity with the other cards.

Next, divide the class into groups, and have each group make four or more similar cards. Let one group at a time share its cards while the rest of the class tries to guess the pictures.

FS123306 Phonics Made Simple—Kindergarten • © Frank Schaffer Publications, Inc.

Name _____

Toy Time

Say the name of each toy. Circle the letter that makes the ending sound. Then color the pictures.

Name_____

A Colorful Quilt

Look at the pictures and color the spaces. Use the code.

Code
word ends in **g** — red word ends in **t** — yellow
word ends in **m** — green word ends in **x** — blue

Name _____

Missing Letters

Write the missing letters for each picture.

__ a __

__ o __

__ a __

__ a __

__ e __

__ o __

__ u __

__ i __

__ i __

__ a __

__ u __

__ e __

64 reproducible FS123306 Phonics Made Simple—Kindergarten • © Frank Schaffer Publications, Inc.

Short Vowels

Learning to hear, read, and write vowel sounds can be a challenging task for children. Since written English is not based on a purely phonetic system (the sound of long *a*, for example, can be written as *ai, ay,* or *ei*), a child can apply the rules of phonics and still misread or misspell a word. Since short vowels are more consistent in their spelling than long vowels, it is best to present them before introducing the other vowel sounds. In kindergarten, children learn to discriminate the short vowels and make beginning attempts at reading and writing short vowel words.

CONCEPTS

The ideas and activities presented in this section will help children develop the following skills:

- identifying short vowel sounds
- distinguishing between two or more short vowels
- distinguishing rhyming words
- reading short vowel words that have a consonant-vowel-consonant pattern

THUMBS UP, THUMBS DOWN *Class Activity*

Let the class practice distinguishing short vowels with this quick game. Tell the students to listen for a particular vowel sound, such as short *a*. Then have the children sit with their hands forming a fist. Next, say several words containing a variety of vowel sounds, such as *lake, can, pine, tube, hand,* and so on. When the students hear you say a short *a* word, they are to flip their thumbs up. For other words, they are to keep their thumbs down. Continue the game for one or two minutes to check vowel discrimination.

MAGNETIC LETTERS *Class Activity*

Let your students practice reading and writing short vowel words with the help of magnetic letters. (Multiple sets will be handy.) Use the letters with a metal cookie tray or a cookie tin lid. If your students are learning short *o* words, for example, begin this activity by forming the word *pot* with the letters. Then call on one student at a time to make a new word by replacing the *p* with another letter. If you like, record the words made on a sheet of chart paper. When several words have been made, continue the activity with another short *o* word ending, such as *-op* or *-ock*.

Short Vowel Collages *Art Project*

Have the class help you make a collage displaying things that have short vowels. For example, if the students are learning the sound of short *i*, have them bring things such as ribbons, rickrack, safety pins, twigs, and other appropriate items, and have the children glue them onto a sheet of butcher paper. Magazine pictures and word cards can also be added to the collage.

FS123306 Phonics Made Simple—Kindergarten ■ © Frank Schaffer Publications, Inc.

The Sound of Short A

LISTEN FOR SHORT "A" *Class Activity*

Say these words, and have the students point out the common sound: *apple, ant, alligator, ask, Ann, Andy*. Then write the words on the chalkboard. Call on students to circle the beginning letters. Have the class see that the letter *a* makes the beginning sound in each word. Tell the class that the sound the *a* makes in these words is called *short a*.

Next, challenge the class to spot the short *a* sound in the following words: *cat, hat, ran, pan, sad, dad*. Guide them into seeing that the vowel sound is in the middle of the word this time. Have the class name other short *a* words, and list their suggestions on a sheet of chart paper.

A SHORT "A" POEM *Class Activity*

Write the following poem on the board:

> An ant ran out of its anthill,
>
> For a snack, for a snack.
>
> He found a little red apple
>
> And ran back, and ran back.

Say the poem one or two times with the students, and have them clap out the beat. Then call on the children to underline the words that have short *a*. Let them recite the poem again, but have them replace *a little red apple* with another phrase that contains the short *a* (examples: *a tasty ham, some toast and jam*).

APPLE TREE CHART *Class Activity*

Have each student cut out two or more apples from red or green paper. On each one, have the children write or illustrate a word that contains short *a*. Then glue the apples onto a sheet of chart paper on which you've drawn a large apple tree.

For an extra challenge, let the students see how many apples they can "pick." Every word or picture that they can name counts as one apple.

Name _____

Help the Ant

Make a path for the ant to get to the anthill. Color the spaces that have pictures of short **a** words.

reproducible 67

The Sound of Short E

LISTEN FOR SHORT "E" *Class Activity*

Tell students to close their eyes and imagine a picture when you say these words: *ten eggs, red pen, wet tent*. Then ask the children to open their eyes and repeat what you said. Write the words on the board. Have the class notice the letter *e* in each word. Tell students that the words all have a short *e* sound.

Next, say several words; as you say each word, have the children say yes if they hear a short *e* sound and no if they do not. Here are some words you might start with: *bike, hen, bed, see, cat, desk, nest, cake, net*.

A SHORT "E" POEM *Class Activity*

Write the following poem on the board:

> When does a hen build a nest for her eggs?
>
> When, can you please tell me when?
>
> When the sun gets up or when the sun sets low?
>
> When, can you please tell me when?

Read the poem to the students. Next, ask them to point out the short *e* words, and call on individual students to underline them. Have the class recite the poem with you. Then have the students make new versions of the poem by replacing the first line with a different one, but challenge them to use as many short *e* words as possible. (Examples: *When does a vet rest from looking at pets? When is it best to go sledding with friends?*)

SHORT "E" RIDDLES *Class Activity*

Make picture cards of these words: *red, ten, vest, tent, web, bell, pen, nest*. Include both the word and the picture. Then read the following riddles, and have your class answer with the correct short *e* word. Display the picture cards as the riddles are answered.

This is a color. (red)

This number comes after nine. (ten)

This is something to wear. (vest)

You can sleep in this when you go camping. (tent)

This is a spider's home. (web)

You write with this. (pen)

This makes a ringing noise. (bell)

A bird lays eggs in this. (nest)

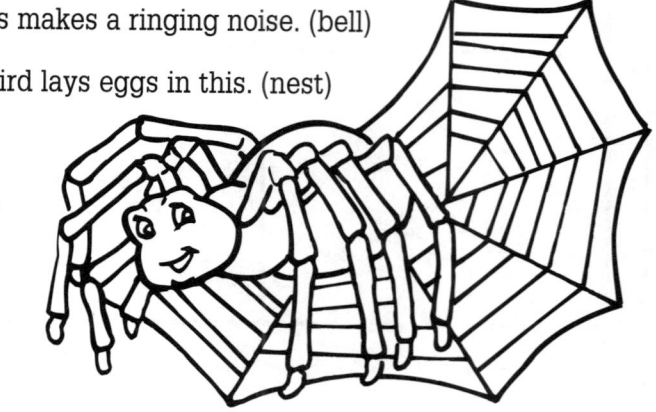

Find the Nest

Help the hen find her nest of eggs. Make a path for her. Color the pictures that have short **e** in their names.

The Sound of Short I

LISTEN FOR SHORT "I"
Class Activity

Ask the students to close their eyes and listen for the common sound in these words: *in, it, is,* and *ill.* Elicit from the class that each word begins with a short *i* sound. Write the words on the chalkboard, and have the students see that the letter *i* makes the beginning sound.

Next, have the students point out the short *i* sound in these words: *pin, sit, list,* and *hill.* Write the words on the board, and call on students to circle the *i*. Then say the following riddles, and have the students guess the short *i* words.

This animal lives in the water. (fish)

This number comes after five. (six)

Babies wear this when they eat. (bib)

You wear this on your hand. (ring)

This word means the opposite of little. (big)

A SHORT "I" POEM
Class Activity

Teach your class the following poem:

A pig in a wig came jiggity-jig,

Jiggity-jig in a big, big wig.

A pig in a wig came jiggity-jig,

What a sight she made—oh, my!

Then have the students replace *pig in a wig* with other short *i* phrases, such as *fish in a dish* or *king with a ring.* For a follow-up activity, have the students illustrate one of the phrases and label their pictures.

SHORT "I" BOOKLETS
Class Activity

Have each student fold a sheet of paper in fourths to make a booklet of short *i* words. On each page, have the student illustrate a short *i* word and label it.

Name _____

Fishing for Short I

Color each fish that has a picture of something that begins with short **i**.

How many fish did you color? _____

The Sound of Short O

WHAT'S IN THE BOX?
Class Activity

Place the following items in a box: a small pot, a doll, a sock, a lock, a toy block, a rock, and a clock. Bring the box to school, and take out the items one at a time. Have students name the items one by one, and have them notice that each word has the same vowel sound. Next, write the words on the board, and have the children see that the letter *o* appears in each one. If you like, add a picture clue beside each word. Then have the students practice saying the short *o* sound by reading the list aloud.

A SHORT "O" POEM
Class Activity

Write the following poem on the board:

> Can you hear a tocking noise?
>
> Tick-a, Tick-a-tock!
>
> It's not a rock, it's not a lock,
>
> It's a ticking-tocking clock!

Have the children recite the poem, and then call on students to underline the words containing short *o*. Later, have the students read the poem again, but have them replace *rock* and *lock* with other short *o* words.

PAIRS OF RHYMING WORDS
Class Activity

Cut out paper socks, and give two socks to each child. Next, have students brainstorm a list of short *o* words that rhyme (examples: *sock, clock; mop, top; log, frog; pot, hot; pod, rod; fox, box*). List the words on the chalkboard. Then have each student choose one pair of words to write or illustrate on the socks. Tell the students to decorate their papers so that the socks in a pair match.

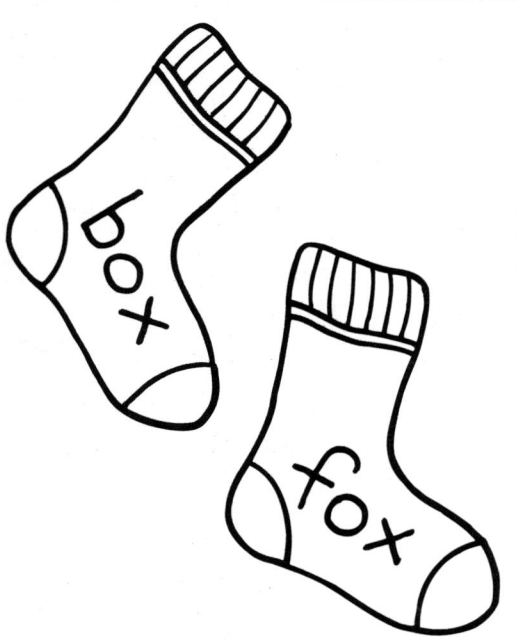

Name _____

Ollie's Words

Draw a line from Ollie's arms to the things that have short **o** in their names. Then color Ollie.

The Sound of Short U

LISTEN AND DO
Class Activity

Have the class listen as you say these words: *up, uncle, us, umbrella, under.* Ask the students what they notice about the words. Then write the words on the board, and have them see that each one begins with the letter *u*. Tell the class that the sound the *u* makes in those words is called *short u*. Have the class say the five words with you and listen to the short vowel.

Next, have the class follow these directions: *Run quietly. Jump on one foot. Hum softly. Rub your hands together.* Then repeat the sentences, and have the students point out the words that have a short *u* sound. Write the words on the board, and call on students to underline the *u* in each one.

A SHORT "U" POEM
Class Activity

Let students recite the following poem to practice saying the short *u* sound:

> Rub-a-dub-dub!
>
> A bug in a tub
>
> Went sailing off one day.
>
> Rub-a-tum-tum!
>
> He started to hum.
>
> He hummed as he sailed away!

Have the children circle the words (including the nonsense words) that contain the short *u* sound. Then have students make up their own nonsense poems using as many short *u* words as they can.

SHORT "U" BUGS
Class Activity

Brainstorm with the class a list of short *u* words. Write the words on the board. Add picture clues beside appropriate words. Then let the students cut out three or more oval shapes from construction paper, and have them copy a short *u* word on each shape. Afterwards, have the students turn their shapes into bugs by adding paper legs, facial features, and decorative markings. Have each child glue his or her shapes onto a large sheet of colored paper.

Name _____

Colorful Umbrellas

Color the umbrellas that have pictures of things with short **u** in their names.

Time to Play

Look at each picture. Say its name. Circle the short vowel you hear.

ANSWER KEY

Page 17
These pictures should be colored: butterfly, bat, book, ball, bell, bag.

Page 19
Lines should be drawn from the cats to the following items: cup, carrot, candle, can, car.

Page 21
These pictures should be colored: doll, duck, door, dice, deer, dinosaur.

Page 23
Lines should be drawn from the fish to the following items: feather, football, fire, fork, fan, five.

Page 25
These pictures should be colored: goat, gate, guitar, girl, garden.

Page 27
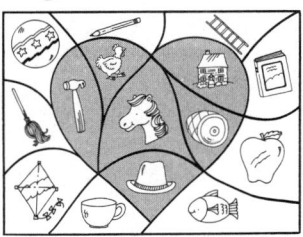

Page 29
The balls with these pictures should be colored: jar, jacks, jug, jumprope, jack-o'lantern, jam.

Page 31
These pictures should be colored: key, kite, kangaroo, kettle, king.

Page 33

Page 35
Lines should be drawn from the mice to the following items: mitten, mushroom, mirror, monkey, mask.

Page 37
Eggs with these pictures should be colored: nail, nine, nut, nickel, needle, necklace, net.

Page 39

Page 41
The spaces with these pictures should be colored yellow: question mark, queen, quilt, quarter, duck quacking. The other spaces should be colored orange.

Page 43
Lines should be drawn from the rabbits to the following items: ribbon, ruler, ring, rain, rake.

Page 45

Page 47

Page 49
These pictures should be colored: vase, violin, vest, volcano, vacuum, van.

Page 51
Lines should be drawn from the worms to the following items: web, watermelon, watch, wallet, wagon, window.

Page 53

Page 55
yarn–yes
key–no
yo-yo–yes
needle–no
yellow crayon–yes
yolk–yes
log–no
yak–yes

Page 57
These pictures should be colored: zigzag line, zebra, zero, zipper, zoo.

Page 58
The following letters should be circled for the corresponding pictures:
lion–l
dog–d
cat–c
bear–b
horse–h
worm–w
yak–y
zebra–z
rabbit–r
turtle–t
kangaroo–k
pig–p

Page 59
The following letters should be circled on the path beside the corresponding pictures:
kite–k
nest–n
table–t
vase–v
bat–b
pear–p
net–n
leaf–l
mittten–m
pencil–p

Page 60
The following letters should be written on the balloons beside the corresponding pictures:
lamp–l
mouse–m
goat–g
pie–p
nail–n
top–t
hammer–h
sock–s
doll–d
ball–b
ruler–r
fish–f

Page 62
The following letters should be circled for the corresponding pictures:
drum–m
ball–l
truck–k
sailboat–t
flag–g
balloon–n
bus–s
top–p
bird–d

Page 63
The spaces with the following pictures should be colored accordingly:
red—dog, bag, pig, flag, frog
green—drum, ham, broom, worm
yellow—cat, net, bat, hat
blue—six, box, ax, fox

Page 64
These words should be completed:
bat, mop, jam
fan, web, dog
jug, pin, six
rat, bus, hen

Page 67
The spaces with the following pictures should be colored: bag, hat, cat, bat, fan, lamp, cap, mask.

Page 71
Fish with these pictures should be colored: pin, mitt, ring, bib, wig, pig.

Page 73
Lines should be drawn from the octopus to the following items: lock, sock, mop, pot, box, clock, top, doll.

Page 75
The umbrellas with these pictures should be colored: cup, bug, rug, truck, bus, sun, jug.

Page 69
The spaces with the following pictures should be colored: pen, net, bed, bell, tent, web, dress, nest.

Page 76
The following letters should be circled for the corresponding pictures:
duck–u
bat–a
block–o
mitt–i
net–e
cat–a
pig–i
truck–u
doll–o
top–o
mask–a
bell–e